Sounds of Disaster

Great Lakes Shipwrecks

by Wes Oleszewski

Avery Color Studios
Marquette, Michigan 49855
1993

Sounds of Disaster
Great Lakes Shipwrecks
by Wes Oleszewski

Copyright 1993
by Avery Color Studios

Library of Congress Card #92-075915
ISBN # 0-932212-76-X
First Edition January 1993
Reprinted 1994

Published by
Avery Color Studios
Marquette, Michigan

Table of Contents

Dedication

To my family.

My wife Teresa, my dad Walt, my mom Sue, sister Jeanine, brother Craig, and all of the in-laws, nieces and nephews that come with them. Your family is who you are, so to these people I give credit for much more than I could ever list. Lucky indeed is the person who can be part of such a loving family.

Glossary

ABEAM—Directly beside a vessel

AFT—Toward the rear of a vessel

BACK—A ship's spine or keel

BARGE—A vessel that has no power of its own and must be towed

BEAM—The width of a vessel

BEAM ENDS—The sides of a vessel

BOAT—On the great lakes, a ship is called a boat

BULKHEAD—A wall-like partition that divides a boat's hull

BUNKER—A compartment where a boat's fuel is stored

CAPSTAN—Device used for pulling lines or chains

FIREHOLD—The part of the engine room where the boiler fires are fed

FO'C'SLE—The raised part of a boat's bow containing crew quarters

FOUNDER—To sink in a disastrous way

FUNNEL—A steamer's smokestack

HAWSER—A tow line, steel or rope

HEEL—To lean to one side

KEEL—A supporting beam that runs the length of a boat's bottom

LIST—A tilt to one side

LIGHTER—To raise a sunken boat by removing its cargo

PORT SIDE—Left side

SALTIE—An ocean going vessel that visits the lakes

SCHOONER-BARGE—A sailing vessel that is usually towed

SCREW—Propeller

SPARDECK—The maindeck through which cargo is loaded

TEXAS DECK—The deck atop which the pilothouse is mounted

YAWL—A small rowboat or lifeboat

Introduction

Along the bottom of all the Great Lakes are littered the remains of hundreds of shipwrecks. Lake Huron alone holds more than 200 historic vessels, like an icewater museum. A few of these lost lakeboats have had the stories of their spectacular disasters told, and told and told again. Many more rest silently forgotten, their stature as a shipwreck not being flamboyant or grisly enough to have their stories told. Still other lakeboats worked successful careers, always bringing their crews home. The adventures of these boats often passed with those who manned them. It is the overlooked adventures of these boats and the people who worked them that will be told in this book.

In my first book, "Stormy Seas—Triumphs and Tragedies of Great Lakes Ships," I attempted to present the more obscure true stories of the lakeboats and their people. More of the same will be found here. In all cases I have attempted to present each narrative in as accurate a format as possible. Trying to tell an accurate tale while avoiding the trappings of "docu-drama" is not an easy task and I often found myself leaving items out that could not be proven to my satisfaction. Additionally, avoiding the creation of a text full of cold data is the other edge of the sword. In all I will claim that this book is not perfect but it is here for your enjoyment and that is why it has been written.

Much was learned from my experience with "Stormy Seas..." For example, writers such as myself can be wrong. In one particular chapter I wrote of a 50-foot wave on Lake Superior. The error was pointed out to me, (post printing), and as any good boat-nut should know, a 50 footer is theoretically possible, but has never happened. Digging through my material I found the 50-foot reference in a sensational headline that I had copied into my notes. On the other hand, a well-known historian published an article in a local newspaper that disputed my time table in the 1924 burning of the steamer MIAMI. Again I returned to my material and found an interview with the vessel's captain upon his return to Bay City immediately after the wreck. With great relief I found that the Captain's time table was exactly the same as mine. On a third front, when researching one of the stories in this book, I fretted for weeks over the position of the vessel (being headed upbound or downbound,) when she came to rest on the bottom. I worried for a month about the condition of the hull of another at the time of her sinking. My concern led to a flurry of long-distance calls to dive shops around lower Michigan, ending with whom I consider to be the premier research diver around the "thumb," David Trotter. Many had said that he may be one of the only persons to have visited these wrecks. Of the first boat he could not recall her position and of the second he simply told me that no one has found her yet. When you think you are going to have historians leaping out to correct you, you find that you are dealing with vessels of great obscurity.

So with chart, dividers, computer, microfilm and library at hand this author has attempted to present accurate, entertaining, true-to-life tales of Great Lakes adventures. It is certain that there will be as many versions of each of these events as there are "historians" to account for them. I present this text to you the reader with the assurance that the tales are true and as close to the actual events as I can manage. What *is* important is that we always keep an open mind and continue always to learn.

A Stylish Patch for the Great Lakes Crazy Quilt

*W*ith the end of the 1800s and the first decade of the 1900s came a fast changing and confused era in Great Lakes shipping. A crazy quilt of different designed oreboats was working the freshwater seas: some were the remnants of days long past, while others were the result of innovative industrial revolution creativity—and some were simply saltwater tramps that had found their way to the lakes. From the wooden lumber hookers to schooners, to the submarine-like whalebacks, the passing of the 1800s had indeed left a wide variety of vessels for the turn-of-the-century boat-watcher to admire.

Wooden vessels such as the "lumber hooker" were constructed out of necessity and convenience. In the early years of Great Lakes maritime commerce, the most abundant boat building material was oak from the sprawling forests surrounding the lakes. These vessels were built of this material in order to carry more of the same to a nation hungry for lumber. Some of the steamers sported the traditional lakeboat profile with pilothouse and officer accommodations mounted forward, engine equipment aft and a clear deck for the cargo hatches, or "spar deck," between. Other lumber hookers had all of their cabins stacked aft with a single mast forward. These lumber hookers were sometimes referred to as "rabbit boats". Most of these wooden steamers averaged 110 to 175 feet in length with shallow depths to suit the shallow boulder-filled rivers leading to the lumber camps. Powerful steam engines were another trait of these lakeboats, allowing for the towing of long strings of wooden barges,

1

sometimes as many as five or more. The barges were unique to the Great Lakes. Once proud sailing schooners found a new lease on life when their rigging was cut down and they were then towed by a lumber hooker. As "schooner-barges" many of these vessels continued to earn their way decades beyond their usefulness as wind-grabbers.

Another vessel unique to the lakes, the "whaleback" was literally dreamed up by Captain Alexander McDougall while master of the steamer HIAWATHA, towing the barges MINNEHAHA and GOSHAWK through tough waters in 1881. Unlike any boat ever before conceived, these had rounded sides and spoon-shaped bows ending in a blunt snout-like peak. The shape was that of a floating cigar with a flat bottom. Captain McDougall's reasoning behind this configuration was to welcome the seas aboard and allow their weight to stabilize the boat and at the same time allow the spoon-shaped bow to follow the line of strain with the least use of rudder. When fully loaded these boats appeared somewhat like a surfaced submarine. Crews were housed below decks or in cabins elevated above the deck atop cylindrical turrets. In another radical departure, Captain McDougall built his whalebacks of steel plate in an era when there were still many who objected to ships made of steel. In keeping with the times, steamers were built as well as companion barges, or "consorts".

With the expansion of the locks at Sault Saint Marie came the steel giants that were the forerunners of today's modern oreboat. Lengths first pushed near and then through the 500 foot mark, and after the turn of the century, 600 feet. The 50s brought 647 foot "super-doopers" and the "maximum size" 730 footer to fit the new St. Lawrence seaway. Almost parallel to this evolution of oreboats was the development of the "self-unloader," with a hopper cargo-hold and a system of conveyor belts running to the end of a boom that could be swung over the side. This system vastly improved the efficiency of lakers and made the self-unloader remarkably handy. With the 1969 dedication of the new 1200 foot long, 110 foot wide, 32 foot deep Poe Lock at the

Showing here style and grace, the C.B. LOCKWOOD passes Mission Point on a pleasant day. Under far different conditions she would confront Lake Erie in the Fall of 1902.

Soo, came the monstrous 1000 foot self-unloader. (All of this had its roots in the pre-1900 industrial revolution.)

Of all the pre-1900 vessel design trends some, such as the "submarine decker" were functional rather than comfortable. The submarine deck arrangement involved the elimination of the aft cabins to allow for the movement of loading and unloading equipment. In these boats the aft deck was raised only a few feet and the crew who resided there were crammed nearly below the water line. The boat's stack, lifeboats and skylight seemed to simply jut up from the stern. Most of the oreboats in this class were around 450 foot and were not popular with crews. On the other hand, some designs were stylish, yet somehow less functional than others. One of these involved placing the forward houses upon the spardeck just aft of the number one hatch. This configuration, augmented by rakish masts and smoke stacks, made for a romantic and eye pleasing appearance, but tended to hinder the latter-day unloading equipment. Thus vessels of this appearance stopped sliding from the shipyards by the end of the 1800s. Such were the lines of the wooden oreboat C. B. LOCKWOOD, and in the crazy quilt era of lakeboats, the LOCKWOOD was unique. With her curving hull sheer, deck-mounted forward houses and three raked masts, she presented the profile of a steel steamer of the era, yet her hull was made of oak timbers. When she came off the ways at Cleveland's Quayle and Son shipyard in 1890, she was one of the largest and most elegant steamers on the Lakes, but within a decade the LOCKWOOD became simply another patch in the oreboat crazy quilt.

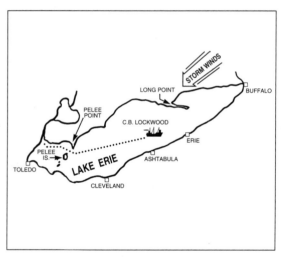

A stylish patch for the Great Lakes Crazy Quilt...

It was a nasty mid-October day in 1902 when Captain Cassius Saph stood peering aft from the square window of his cabin on board the C. B. LOCKWOOD. Behind him, seated in a comfortable chair and wrapped in her favorite shawl, the Captain's wife was doing a bit of reading. Captain Saph was keeping a casual watch on First Mate John Fritz, who was in turn supervising the loading of 3000 tons of flax consigned to Buffalo. The LOCKWOOD's 292 foot size was only marginally competitive in the 1902 iron ore market, but in the coal and grain markets, she could earn her way. At the moment, Captain Saph's employers, the J. C. Gilchrist Company, had their fleet in the thick of the annual fall grain rush. Every elevator on the Lakes was in an urgent hurry to ship their grain east before winter's ice locked the channels tight. Captain Saph knew that these grain runs were all a part of Gilchrist's philosophy of operating their boats at maximum profit with minimum expense. This was the same reason why the LOCKWOOD like her cargo, and the Gilchrist fleet, was uninsured.

Before the last hatchplank was in place and while the tarps were still being stretched across the closed hatches, Captain Saph had headed his boat across Duluth Harbor toward Lake Superior. By the time John Fritz got to the pilothouse to report the hatches secure, Captain Saph was guiding the LOCKWOOD onto the open lake. The weather was cold and gray with a brisk wind and an ice water chop slapping against the LOCKWOOD's wooden bow. Meteorology was of little concern to Captain Saph. It was a typical October day on Superior, the kind that he had seen many times before. Weather aside, the LOCKWOOD, although not spanking new, was at 12 seasons old barely broken in by wooden lakeboat standards. So, into the early dusk and ill-tempered Lake Superior Captain Saph hauled the LOCKWOOD.

By dawn on Sunday, October 12, 1902, a respectable gale was blowing across Lakes Superior, Michigan, and Huron. Waves quickly turned into rolling hills of blue-gray water, and with the wind came sleet, spitting against the boat and freezing instantly. Many of the smaller vessels and their consorts took shelter, but most boats simply snored ahead and wallowed through the mess. This was, for the most part, just another October storm. At Port Huron, the C. B. LOCKWOOD came chugging off Lake Huron as if to shrug off the storm and its precipitation. For most of Sunday afternoon and night the wooden steamer slid down the swift waters of the St. Clair River. Even in summer's calm dog days, avoiding the steady parade of upbound boats was no easy task. In the storm winds and rain mixed with sleet of an

October storm, each turn of the river and appearance of another upbounder presented a hazard to the downbound LOCKWOOD.

There was no sunset that Sunday night, the darkness just sinking upon the LOCKWOOD like slow death as she pushed across Lake St. Clair. There the wind and waves tossed the shallow water into another nasty chop. Along the shore, families spent a snug Sunday night in their large homes, as from each chimney smoke rose and was ripped away by the damp wind. Moving from the glow of their fireplaces, St. Clair residents could normally see the string of amber lights belonging to the vessels out on the lake, but not on this stormy night in 1902. The rain and sleet prevented that. Although storm-whipped, the crew of the LOCKWOOD, at least those not on deck, were far from uncomfortable. One thing that a steamer has is an abundance of heat. As long as her boilers could make steam to be piped through the radiators, her cabins would be warmed.

Through the pre-dawn hours of Monday the 13th, Captain Saph guided his stylish wooden steamer down the Detroit River and into Lake Erie. There he found the storm winds still blowing. The LOCKWOOD began to pitch and roll with the seas even before she cleared Bar Point and the river's confines. Her timbers moaned faintly as the good Captain ordered her swung onto a Buffalo track. The boat would haul south, southeast on a 150 degree course and look for Middle Sister Island, then turn nearly due east and run the 20 miles to Pelee Island. Threading Pelee Passage between the island to the south and the point to the north would be the most difficult task of the trip, but it was a chore that the LOCKWOOD and her crew had accomplished many times before. Once clear of the passage, the wheelsman would steer a 071 degree course to steam the more than 100 storm-raked miles to Long Point. From there another ten degrees toward north would put her on a Buffalo way in just over 50 miles. With the wind quartering on her stern the LOCKWOOD would take some water, and twist a bit, but would make good time. Without regard to the boat's motion, Captain Saph retired to his cabin as soon as Pelee Passage was clear, the weather and rivers having kept him from sleep since Lake Huron.

The C. B. LOCKWOOD had spent a nasty day pounding toward Buffalo, rolling and twisting, decks awash all the way. Shortly before sundown, Captain Saph was awakened by a change in the roll of the wooden deck below his bed. Every instinct screamed at the LOCKWOOD's master, but his common sense told him to wait for another wave. As the boat rolled from the next wave, a shock rolled up Captain Saph's spine, pulled at his ears and brought a cold tingle to his brow. The LOCKWOOD was growing sluggish in the seas, and that could mean only one thing—the boat was leaking and leaking badly. First Mate Fritz was sent aft to inspect the hatch tarps and have the chief start the pumps. By the time the soaked mate got to the engine room, the syphons were already running and had already been over-whelmed by the in-rushing lake. Worse yet, the fires that heated the LOCKWOOD's boilers were being threatened by the filthy water that was filling the firehold. Wherever the leak was, it was massive in nature. Mate Fritz knew now what Captain Saph's instinct had told him a half hour before—the LOCKWOOD was sinking.

Captain Saph estimated his position off Ashtabula, Ohio when the fires went out. All hands mustered aft atop the stern deckhouse and prepared to launch the yawls. The Captain directed that mate Fritz would take command of one lifeboat with nine of the LOCKWOOD's crew. Captain Saph would take the other with his wife, Mrs. Davis, the ship's cook and six others aboard. Lake Erie now took hold of the steamer, wind-locking her in the sea trough and sweeping her off course toward the south. Winds shrieked in gusts through her rigging, like the howling ghost of death poised to take all in its way without a trace.

Meanwhile on Lake Superior, another pair of patches in the oreboat crazy quilt were playing out a bit of drama. Downbound and filled with iron ore was the Pittsburgh Steamship Company's

452 foot steel steamer MAUNALOA. Interestingly, the MAU-NALOA, although slightly longer and made of steel, had almost the same profile as the LOCKWOOD. Deep inside her hull however, her builders at the Chicago Shipbuilding Company had installed a powerful quadruple expansion steam engine. For this reason she often towed a barge, and on this fitful October afternoon the MAUNALOA had a unique consort tied to her stern. Nearly four boat lengths behind the steamer and fastened with a thick steel towing hawser was the whaleback barge 129. Even in calm waters, when loaded, the whalebacks rode with only a few feet of their hull sticking above the surface, giving indeed the appearance of a surfaced whale's back. The only difference was the turret-like deck houses mounted on the bow and stern. Barge 129, running on stormy Lake Superior, was today putting Captain McDougall's theory to work. From the pilothouse of the MAUNALOA, it was at times nearly impossible to see Barge 129, which was swamped and buried by each wave. The whaleback was stable, but for the MAUNALOA, the experience was much the same as towing a giant log.

Both vessels had slogged through the storm with little complaint until they were 40 miles from rounding Whitefish Point. Barely audible over the fitful storm, a dull boom, like a distant cannon shot, drew the attention of the MAUNALOA's crew. The wallowing whaleback was already falling off her heading and the stress of the wind and seas had parted the steel hawser, Barge 129 was adrift and at Superior's mercy.

Now the MAUNALOA would have to turn in a wide arc and back-track through the storm to attempt to re-moor its drifting barge. Finding the wayward whaleback was no easy task, with only its turret deck houses sticking above the rolling surface, but within an hour, the MAUNALOA had returned to Barge 129. Atop the whaleback's forward turret, two shivering and drenched crewmen were prepared to take the new line. On the fantail and fo'c'sle of the MAUNALOA, crew members were ready to pass the hawser, when without warning, the steamer slid toward the barge, crashing into it with a sickening scream and inflicting a mortal gash in its submerged hull.

Without hesitation, the crew of Barge 129 made for the yawl, which was suspended aft of the stern turret. Launching the boat was a numbing scramble for survival. The whaleback was going down beneath their feet as the crew took to the boat. Minutes later, the entire crew of Barge 129 was aboard the MAUNALOA and the whaleback was plummeting through more than 400 feet of water to the bottom of Lake Superior. MAUNALOA sailed on into the stormy afternoon, making the Soo with her survivors in good shape, but leaving Barge 129 to rest forever on Superior's bottom.

On Lake Erie the once proud wooden steamer C. B. LOCK-WOOD was taking her final mortal blows from the merciless sea. Over the shouts, squeaking davits and howling wind, it was impossible to keep track of each lifeboat that had been lowered. There in the maelstrom, the yawls became separated from one another, and First Mate John Fritz's boat wallowed from sight into the waves. No one saw the LOCKWOOD go down. They were simply too busy trying to stay atop the waves, and the steamer was lost in the spume.

Captain Saph's yawl was in trouble, for shortly after it hit the churning water, one of the two oars was plucked away by the lake. In the scramble of numbed hands to recover the oar, one of the crewmen made the mistake of getting too close to the pro-voked lake and was grabbed and pulled overboard. A moment later he found himself thrashing about in Lake Erie's frigid boil. With the use of the remaining oar and the hands of his ship-mates, he was rescued from the lake's ice water clutches. Brought back aboard the yawl, trembling uncontrollably, he wondered if he hadn't glimpsed the fate that awaited them all.

Necessity is the mother of invention, but desperation is both the parents of survival. With these premises at heart, Captain Saph looked around the nearly swamped lifeboat and quickly devised a scheme for survival. The single oar was lashed forward like a mast and the Captain's wife was asked to surrender her large, warm shawl, which was then rigged as a sail. Away with the wind ran the tiny lifeboat and her crew of nine, sailing before a storm that had just beaten a 292 foot steamboat to death.

Somehow, either by fate or divine Providence, the 366 foot oreboat G. J. GRAMMER, headed for Ashtabula, came upon the tiny yawl. The spotlight from the big, brand-new steel steamer illuminated a frantic scene as it landed upon the castaways. Some were bailing for the lives of all, some were shivering and nearly unconscious, and everyone who was able beckoning—as if in fear that the big steamer would for some reason pass them by. Hours later, the GRAMMER was moored snugly at her unloading berth in Ashtabula, and the survivors of the LOCKWOOD were recovering well, thanks to the GRAMMER's captain and crew. Mate John Fritz's yawlboat was lost with all hands. It simply rowed off into the storm and took ten lives with it.

Today, the bottom of the Great Lakes is a crazy quilt of shipwrecks, from schooners to whalebacks to straightdeck giants, much the same as its surface was in 1902. If one could take away all of the water just for a moment, and oversee all of the vessels resting below, he might just notice, 13 miles off Fairport Harbor, the old C. B. LOCKWOOD, just one obscure but unique patch in the crazy quilt of oreboats gone by.

The Ghost Ship
of Yankee Reef

*L*ate season navigation on the Great Lakes has never been a picnic, for the months of November and December are always storm-filled. Fast-marching pockets of low pressure bring cyclonic winds of hurricane strength from the Canadian plains. They come to agitate the lakes into an icy rage and to torment those forced to work upon them. Following these lows come winds of Arctic cold air that can turn the water into a solid sheet of ice in hours. Luckless freighters can find themselves frozen in port while trying to get that "one last cargo of the season". In modern times, powerful Coast Guard icebreakers keep freezing channels open. Weather satellites keep careful track of approaching storms, beaming their images directly into a boat's pilothouse. The giant lakeboats keep hauling, well into January. Things were vastly different in 1891 as Captain Edward Ballentine brought the 200 foot wooden steamer ELFIN MERE up Saginaw Bay. All that a master of vessels had for aid in this era was a barometer and his own sense of the weather.

"King lumber" was the product that kept the lakeboats earning a profit in this era and the ELFIN MERE was in the middle of the Great Lakes lumber boom. From the Michigan ports of Saginaw, Tawas, Au Sable, Alpena and the like, log product was produced at a rate of over four billion board-feet in 1883. The Saginaw and Tittabawassee Rivers were normally choked with logs, the riverbank docks stacked with cut board three stories high. From the mid 1850s to the early 1880s it appeared as if the timber in central Michigan could never be exhausted. By 1884 however, the forests of the Saginaw Valley had been ravaged to the point where the lumberjacks could no longer float enough logs down the rivers to keep Saginaw's mills profitable. As a solution lake schooners and steamers were employed to haul logs and rough-cut timber down from northern Michigan and the Canadian shore along Georgian Bay. Surely those endless expanses of timber would never run out.

Hauling down lumber was the ELFIN MERE's task as she beat her way across Saginaw Bay. It was Thursday morning November 26th, 1891 and a nasty late season gale had been howling from the south through the night. As the storm's center passed toward central western Ontario, the winds on Lake Huron kept up their cyclonic pattern and shifted to the southwest. This caused the Michigan mainland to block some of the storm winds and allowed navigation across Saginaw Bay and western Lake Huron. Captain Ballentine found the seas still rolling high and the winds continuing to blow a storm. It seemed to him simply another autumn blow, like so many he had weathered before. He had no inkling that just over the horizon this storm would call for some maneuvering that was about to make heroes of him and his crew.

The night before Captain Ballentine pushed his boat out to meet the wind and waves, another wooden lakeboat had done the same from the port of Alpena, Michigan. Towing a string of three schooner-barges, the 135 foot lumber steamer OSWE-GATCHIE beat her way onto Thunder Bay. Following faithfully behind came the barges McBRIER, N. P. GOODELL and H. C. POTTER, all with decks stacked high with northern Michigan's lumber. Meeting the four was a fresh southeast gale, and the OSWEGATCHIE's master regretted leaving Alpena's shelter as soon as the first waves hit his bow. Turning to run back to Alpena would be prevented by the OSWEGATCHIE's string of barges. A 180 degree turn would expose the tow to the sea trough causing each boat to roll and cork-screw. The resulting stress of the rolling boats would part the towing hawser in minutes, setting the lot adrift at the bidding of the lake. Considering the alternatives, the OSWEGATCHIE had no choice other than steaming on, head to the seas.

Through the evening Wednesday and into the darkness of Thursday morning the storm increased in its violence. Wave after wave smashed against the OSWEGATCHIE's bow in an

This rare photo shows the OSWE-GATCHIE in her early career. Later she would be cut down to carry "King Lumber" and would soon become one of the forgotten wrecks of Lake Huron.

COURTESY MILWAUKEE PUBLIC LIBRARY MARINE COLLECTION

unending attack. It was a constant fight just to keep the steamer's head to the wind and seas. The working of her 24-year-old hull planks wore against her calking as each wave twisted the hull. During the night, water began to seep into her hold and was quickly discovered by First Mate Marsillot. As her timbers worked with the seas, her calking was giving way. Checking of the boat's speed would slow the action and give her pumps a chance to work. In this effort, her master checked the steamer's revolutions down until the wooden lakeboat was just able to keep her head to the seas, and waited for the syphons to do their job.

Screaming across the bay, the winds were so strong that through the night the four boats had made no more than 35 miles since leaving Alpena. For hours the quartet were held in place in the pre-dawn blackness as the gale worked them over. The seas came like an endless gray-capped washboard, melting into the snow-obscured horizon. Normally, checking the steamer down would have worked to the end that her master intended, but as the night passed the winds intensified further. Now the OSWEGATCHIE was starting to blow around and her steam engine had to be throttled up to full ahead once more. Come what may, the lumber carrier would have no alternative other than charging "full ahead" into the fury.

An hour before dawn First Mate Marsillot went down into the OSWEGATCHIE's creaking hold to make another check on the water that was continuing to seep into her. There was no need to hold his lantern close to the timbers to evaluate the seams because the water was as high as his waist. Balancing himself against the oak bulkhead, the startled mate stood hip-deep in

The OSWEGATCHIE and her string of barges.

– Author's Concept

the sloshing icewater. The glow of his lamp showed Lake Huron gushing through nearly every seam that the cargo would allow him to see. Clearly, the boat's pumps had been overwhelmed and the OSWEGATCHIE was now sinking.

Unknown to those aboard the OSWEGATCHIE, the schooner-barges that she towed were not faring much better. All were being swept constantly by the seas and a good portion of their deck cargos had gone over the side. Worst off was the 119 foot schooner-barge N. P. GOODELL. The incessant buffeting on the barge's 224 ton oak hull had caused her seams to part like those of the OSWEGATCHIE. For hours the GOODELL's crew had been working the hand pumps, but the 27-year-old schooner had already given up. In her hold the water steadily gained and her sole hope was that the OSWEGATCHIE could somehow pull them off the fitful lake.

Shortly after noon the intruding lake found the OSWE-GATCHIE's engine room and before long set upon her fires and snuffed them out. From her funnel the belches of black smoke were agonizingly replaced by a surge of filthy steam. This was the death stroke for the steamer and spelled the fate of her barges. By then the winds had shifted to the southwest and had moderated a bit. Onboard the OSWEGATCHIE everyone knew that the only chance for the barges was to cut them loose giving them the chance to make it on their own. Each of the schooners immediately cut loose from one another and their crews went to work setting their sails. As the wind shifted more to the west, it began to snow hard and soon all four boats were only intermittently visible to each other.

Getting at least one sail up, the McBRIER turned and vanished among the snow squalls. The POTTER got her canvas up, and like cannon fire, the winds promptly blew it to shreds. Now the 308 ton schooner-barge was left simply to blow before the winds, and she too was swallowed by the snow. With decks nearly awash the GOODELL took to her sails and likewise had them blown out. The mass of her water-logged hull kept her from blowing away from the OSWEGATCHIE as rapidly as the others. Instead she sat there like the steamer— waiting to sink. Scattered by the winds off Sturgeon Point, all four boats were now completely at Lake Huron's mercy.

Onboard the ELFIN MERE, Captain Ballentine was having a difficult time seeing through the intensified snow. Hugging as close as he dared to the Michigan shore, the captain was looking to get as much lee from the land as possible. The winds continued to blow a storm, but were beginning to swing due west as the ELFIN MERE approached the boulder-studded waters south of Sturgeon Point. For a moment the snow squalls broke and across the heaving seas Captain Ballentine spotted a number of vessels. It struck the captain that this was a lot of traffic to be crowding the waters in such stormy weather. As the snow swept across the scene once more, Captain Ballentine realized that he had seen a distressed steamer and what remained of her tow.

Navigating instinctively the captain moved in the direction of the closest of the vessels. As the snow again parted Captain Ballentine caught sight of one of the distressed vessels. Wallowing low by the stern was the OSWEGATCHIE dead in the waves. At the steamer's stern, her desperate crew were preparing to launch the yawl. Dropping the schooner she had been towing, the ELFIN MERE circled the leeward side of the OSWEGATCHIE, all the while trying to avoid the mass of drifting lumber that had been washed from her deck cargo. A single plank from this flotsam could easily foul the steamer's screw or rudder putting her too at the mercy of the lake. Taking the boat's wheel Captain Ballentine eased his steamer's beam across the OSWE-GATCHIE's sinking stern. With a bump and loud crunching, the waves ground the two boats together. One after another the crew of the OSWEGATCHIE jumped for their lives. The entire scene was a strange contrast—the ELFIN MERE in her most glorious moment and the OSWEGATCHIE in her most sorrowful.

After successfully rescuing the endangered crew the ELFIN MERE gingerly pulled away and went to pick up her consort. In the distance only the GOODELL could still be seen, sunk nearly to her rails, her sails blown out and lifeboat washed away. The poor schooner-barge was trapped in the sea trough and rolling on her beam ends. That west wind had her now and was rapidly blowing her out onto the open lake. So high were the waves in her area that Captain Ballentine knew that there was no way he could get the ELFIN MERE to her. All that those aboard the ELFIN MERE could do was watch as the storm and the lake took the GOODELL away.

The Ghost Ship of Yankee Reef.

A close run along the Michigan shore kept the ELFIN MERE out of Lake Huron's clutches. At seven that evening, the rescue steamer and the OSWEGATCHIE's castaways came rolling into Alpena. There they told how the lake had beaten down the OSWEGATCHIE and carried away her consorts. One after another, they seemed to agree that the three schooners and all of those aboard were lost. By midnight the speculation about the lost trio of schooner-barges was still running high around the

Alpena water front. It was then that a pair of amber lamps from a single schooner were seen on Thunder Bay plying toward Alpena. As a ghost would return from the beyond, the schooner-barge McBRIER heeled into port. Her fight against the storm to make the distance from Sturgeon Point to Alpena had taken just under 12 hours. She arrived nearly a wreck, but her crew safe.

Witnessing the McBRIER's return from the dead, famed Alpena vesselman Frank W. Gilchrist mustered a crew of volunteers and prepared his steambarge GARDEN CITY for sailing. The task of the 140 foot wooden steamer tonight would not be her normal toil of lumber hauling, but would instead be the search for mariners in distress. Certainly if the McBRIER had survived, the GOODELL and POTTER might still be afloat. By the time the GARDEN CITY was ready to sail, the wind and pelting snow were still too powerful to allow her out onto Lake Huron. Not until 4 o'clock in the morning did the searching steamer battle out onto Thunder Bay. The winds had died nearly to a northwest bluster but the seas on the open lake were still running high and the snow came down heavily. As the GARDEN CITY crashed through one wave after another, the crew stood a numbing vigil at her rails, showered by each exploding sea.

At first light the big schooner MARION W. PAGE came running across Thunder Bay tacking through the snow. Her 202 foot wooden hull was packed with 1500 tons of coal from Huron, Ohio, bound to Chicago. All the way up Lake Huron the wind jammer had made bad weather of it, but now just off North Point the lake got the better of her. Through the snow squalls the schooner's master saw the shore, where he did not expect it. There was no room to move and nothing he could do, other than watch, as the spike of North Point reached out and speared the PAGE. Luck was with the schooner as the surf was only moderate, so the boat's wooden hull was not working badly against the shore, and the boat settled firmly with little damage to her planks. With the current winds, the PAGE might just hold up until help could be sent from Alpena. Until then the crew would just sit in the cabin and wait, like turkeys in the coop on Thanksgiving eve.

As Lake Huron's irritated surface was illuminated by the belated dawn, the GARDEN CITY continued to search. Spray from the seas had accumulated in the form of ice upon her hull, rigging and crew, yet there had been no sight of any of the missing vessels. In a wide zigzag pattern, the little wooden steamer pressed her search across the western lake and down toward Saginaw Bay. From the warmth of the GARDEN CITY's octagon pilothouse, Mr. Gilchrist scanned the snow-obscured horizon for any sign of the missing lakeboats, when there came a shout from the deck—an object had been sighted among the seas.

Just four miles north of Sturgeon Point and three miles from shore, the prow of a vessel jutted between the waves. As the GARDEN CITY drew near the wreck it quickly became obvious that they had found the OSWEGATCHIE. The wreck's position was quite remarkable. She sat with her stern rail resting on the bottom, anchored by the weight of her boilers. With her stern on the bottom and buoyed up by the air trapped in her bow, the OSWEGATCHIE sat pointing straight up with her peak 15 foot out. For a long while the GARDEN CITY hovered near the sunken lumber hooker. Those onboard the search boat gazed at the sight with astonishment. It was an odd posture indeed for a steamer to be in. When their amazement had abated, the thought that the wreck might be towed into shallower water was considered. Butting up against the sunken OSWEGATCHIE, the GARDEN CITY put a line over and pulled at the wreck. Tugging with all she had the GARDEN CITY could not budge the wreck. At length the line was let go and the GARDEN CITY plowed back for Alpena to report her findings. Left behind, the OSWE-GATCHIE continued to stand on her tail as if reluctant to succumb to Lake Huron's ultimate will.

A day had passed since the OSWEGATCHIE's tow had been set adrift and nothing had been seen or heard from the POTTER or GOODELL. Around the Lake Huron port cities the talk was all about the two familiar schooner-barges. Many people were sure that the two were the latest to be devoured crew and all by the lake. Eye witnesses aboard the OSWEGATCHIE and ELFIN MERE swore that the lifeboats of both schooner-barges had been washed away long before they had gone astray. As a result, the crews of both boats were trapped aboard with no means of escape.

Entering Alpena the GARDEN CITY passed the tug RALPH that was outbound onto Thunder Bay. By two o'clock that afternoon Mr. Gilchrist had his lumber hooker tied up and the tug FRANK W. was also on its way out. Chugging toward North Point, the two tugs were on their way to aid the stranded schooner MARION W. PAGE. When the tug RALPH reached the scene the schooner was found to be in good condition. She was leaking a bit as would be expected, so the RALPH hoisted aboard a steam pump, then went to hauling on the distressed wind grabber. With remarkable ease the PAGE slipped from the point and floated free. Approaching the area, the FRANK W. apparently had been beaten out of a towing commission, as the PAGE appeared ready to sail on to Chicago. Discussions with the schooner's master found him unwilling to sail her through the Straits of Mackinac in her current leaking condition. After a short bidding war the FRANK W. found herself employed in an escort tow into Lake Michigan. For both tugs it had been a profitable afternoon.

Late Friday evening the fishing tug MAXWELL A. made Alpena and her crew wasted no time in excitedly passing on their news. While steaming through the persisting snow nearly in the middle of Lake Huron off Big Reef, which in modern times is called Yankee Reef, the tug spotted what appeared to be a distressed schooner. The MAXWELL A. pulled near the derelict, thinking that there was a crew that would need rescuing. A sad and strange sight is what they found wallowing atop the reef. It was the GOODELL, sunken nearly to her rails, with canvas and rigging torn away as well as the yawl. Circling the barge, the crew of the tug hailed over to her, but no response came. Blowing the tug's whistle went without response. Then a strange observation was made. A large portion of what remained of the schooner-barge's deck cargo of lumber was clearly burned. Apparently a desperate crew had set the lumber ablaze in order to attract the attention of a passing vessel. Concluding that the wreck was resting safely upon the reef, and that there were no souls aboard, the MAXWELL A. headed on toward Alpena. Since there was no way that the tiny fishing tug could tow the water-logged schooner, especially in the prevailing weather, there was nothing more to do.

Returning from her escort of the MARION W. PAGE through the straits, the tug FRANK W. got word of the GOODELL. Hungry for another dividend, the tug made for mid-lake at full steam. The position of the schooner-barge given by the fishing tug was 47 miles below the Thunder Bay light, but when the FRANK W. got to that area, they found nothing. From horizon to horizon, there was only the choppy gray surface of Lake Huron blending into the snow. Apparently those aboard the MAXWELL A. had been wrong when they concluded that the GOODELL was sitting on the reef. Obviously, the water there was too deep to fetch the waterlogged barge, and she had drifted away. The FRANK W. headed back toward Alpena, empty-handed.

Saturday night, while the FRANK W. was still out in search of missing vessels, the plight of the OSWEGATCHIE, her barges and their missing crews were being overshadowed by events in Alpena. Bound for Milwaukee from Buffalo came the 200 foot wooden steamer ARIZONA towing the 220 foot schooner-barge PLYMOUTH. Both boats were loaded to the hilt with hard coal and hauling through the snow squalls. While attempting to hug as close as possible to the lee of the shore, the pair had lined up on a 295 degree course. By all rights this should have put them just below Bois Blanc Island in just under 10 hours. Instead, a little more than an hour after the pair made their turn, the jut of Presque Isle reached out and snagged them both at nearly the same instant. Once more the GARDEN CITY steamed to the rescue, this time accompanied by the tug RALPH. It was with the hope that they could pull the ARIZONA and PLYMOUTH free, before another late fall tantrum could sweep across the lake.

Alpena telegraphs clicked frantically with a flash of marine news from down on Lake Erie, about the schooner-barge TAILOR tied up in Buffalo. It had been the last trip of the season for the wooden boat when she was caught on open Lake Erie by the snowy gale. Suddenly, late Thursday night the barge was blown onto her beam ends and sacked by a series of seas. The result of both actions caused her deck cargo to cascade over the side. Sailor James Bradley was caught on deck at the moment the cargo went over and was lost into Lake Erie as well. This was a sorrowful way for the TAILOR and her crew to end the 1891 season.

At Cheboygan, Michigan, Captain Stephen B. Grummond's wrecking tug LEVIATHAN caught fire and went adrift down the river. On board her crew fought desperately to contain the flames, but the LEVIATHAN was determined to incinerate. To the rescue came the tug STRNAN tossing a line to the choking crew and pulling the flaming tug to the river bank. As soon as the LEVIATHAN's burning hulk slammed ashore, her crew leaped for safety, tumbling one after another into the snow, as showers of glowing embers rained all around. Standing covered with clumps of sooty snow clinging to their smoke-saturated clothing, the crewmen could only watch as the LEVIATHAN, the expensive steam pumps and all of her wrecking equipment were destroyed.

Down at Bay City Captain Henry Dawson brought the tug WITCH OF THE WEST up to the Young Brothers coal dock. It was a stop that for Captain Dawson was far beyond routine. Coal from the Young Brothers dock was simply fuel and their pay rate often drew the tug there. As loading began, Captain Dawson was in the dock office attempting to shake off the cold that the recent storm had left behind. Without doubt, the conversation speculated over the end of the OSWEGATCHIE and the fate of the missing barges GOODELL and POTTER as well as the crews. All of the boats were regular visitors to the Saginaw River and Captain Dawson and his tug had often worked them. From the dock came an unexpected commotion, a chorus of shouts followed by the crashing of equipment. Craning toward the office window Captain Dawson could see members of the tug's crew scrambling to the dock. Stumbling over an assortment of office furniture, the captain bounded toward his ship, arriving just in time to watch the listing tug sink slowly to the river bottom. Geysers of air and water shot from every opening as the tug settled on her side. It did not take much investigation to find that coal fuel had been loaded on one side of the bunker, causing the WITCH OF THE WEST to heel over, and allowing water to intrude through one of the syphons. All that Captain Dawson could do now was stand on the wharf, with the fuel requisition in one hand and pencil in the other, watching as his possessions and those of his crew popped to the surface and drifted away on the Saginaw River.

Captain Dawson's possessions were still floating away when Lake Huron returned another floating object. At the tip of Michigan's thumb just off Point aux Barques, the missing schooner-barge H. P. POTTER of the OSWEGATCHIE's tow came drifting toward shore, pushed by the wind that was blowing from nearly due north. Seeing the stricken schooner-barge nearing from off the choppy lake, the local lifesavers prepared for a major rescue. As the POTTER came crashing upon the rocky shore the lifesavers launched their surfboat and pulled for the wreck. Rowing under the lee of the beaten schooner's hull, the surfmen shouted to her crew, but there was no response. Thinking that the POTTER's crew might be suffering from the cold and unable to respond, the surfmen put a line aboard and climbed onto the barge. What they found was a sight. All the POTTER's rigging had been blown down and littered the deck. Her deck cargo had been pillaged by the lake to the point where there were only remnants scattered about. Below in the partially-flooded hold the main cargo was intact. The boat's yawl with its equipment had obviously been bitten away by Lake Huron. In her fo'c'sle and after cabins there was only the sloshing possessions of the crew. Returning to shore, the surfmen reported that after having searched every corner of the ice cold cabins, there was no sign of her crew or where they had gone. Promptly a wire was sent to Alpena to announce the POTTER's fetching up. Once more the tug FRANK W. was dispatched to attempt a recovery.

Meanwhile, up on Presque Isle, first the barge PLYMOUTH and later the lumber hooker ARIZONA were pulled free. At about this same time a pair of welcome messages came into Alpena. The H. P. POTTER's crew had turned up at Detroit, apparently picked up by a passing vessel. The crew of the GOODELL were at Bayfield, Ontario having burned that portion of the schooner's deck cargo and managing to alert a passing vessel. They were badly frost-bitten, but quite safe. There was only one loose end left by the storm— the GOODELL was still missing.

Today only stumps remain from that great lumber era, and only fragments of records remain of the wooden lakeboats that served "king lumber." The McBRIER sailed again, but the POTTER was simply too beaten to work anymore. As of this writing, 100 years nearly to the day after the storm, the OSWEGATCHIE rests on the bottom of Lake Huron just off Sturgeon Point. Remarkably, no one has yet found her sleeping hulk. She waits in obscurity as modern day water skiers, sport fishermen and boaters ply overhead. A century after she was last seen on what is now Yankee Reef, the schooner-barge GOODELL has yet to be found. Perhaps because no lives were lost in the OSWE-GATCHIE's wreck the events were long forgotten. So it is important to remember that while you read this tale, the ghost ship N. P. GOODELL, with her deck cargo partly burned in a call for help, never came in off Lake Huron. Possibly while touring the Huron coast you may catch a glimpse of a beaten schooner-barge that is there and then gone. Perhaps you have just seen the ghost ship of Yankee Reef, but then again...perhaps not.

Toward the
Sounds of Disaster

*N*ight's fog had formed steadily yet slowly over the St. Marys River. From their tower high above the Soo Locks the lock tenders watched as one after another the lakeboats appeared upbound and downbound through the hanging mist. Finally the visibility was reduced to the point where only portions of boats locking through could be clearly seen. Those at the Soo squinted toward each glowing of upbound amber lights with growing expectation. A spanking new oreboat was expected up on her maiden trip tonight, and most of the Soo's boat watchers had been waiting since late Sunday evening for her passage. Finally, near midnight, the probing beams of two searchlights split the fog, as the amber blobs that they emanated from approached the lower locks. It was now Monday morning July 12, 1909, an era before marine radio, Soo Control, channel 14, and a definite order of vessel traffic. Vessels navigated on their own accord and held for weather at their master's discretion. Positive identification of the two boats now approaching the locks was possible only when they loomed close enough through the fog to read their names.

As the first of the two upbounders became clear, through the mist the name ISAAC M. SCOTT was clearly painted on her bow. She was the brand new boat that everyone had been waiting for, and directly behind her came the FRANK H. GOODYEAR. As the SCOTT's 524 foot hull slid toward the open lock, Captain Archie McArthur stood watching over her darkened pilothouse. The M. A. Hanna Company operated the SCOTT and had seen fit to give her to Captain McArthur right out of the yard. Bringing his new boat up the Detroit and St.Clair Rivers and northward on Lake

Huron, the proud master had answered salutes all the way. Surely this was the beginning of a long and fruitful career, despite the delay caused by a little pea soup fog at the Soo. In less than a half hour the SCOTT was pushing her way from the lock, her spotlight darting along the lock approach. Following in the SCOTT's wake the FRANK H. GOODYEAR prepared for her long trek to Duluth. Slowly the two oreboats were blended together by the fog until they were again just amber blobs, and shortly there after swallowed by the fog.

The SCOTT was delivered to the Virginia Steamship Company, so when she passed the Soo her stack did not sport the star and "H" of Hanna's giant fresh water fleet. Naturally, this meant little to her crew or to the boat-watchers ashore, for tonight she was simply the newest boat on the lakes. It was a title, that in the first decade of the 1900s was as long-lasting as the fog she was sailing into.

Onboard the FRANK H. GOODYEAR, Captain Russell Hemenger kept a sharp eye on the lights of the SCOTT, and a sharp ear on her whistle. In this era before radar, his best aid to navigation through the fog would be his compass, clock, and the SCOTT. He needed just to keep her lights in sight while at the same time watching his own course. Oncoming boats would be first visible to the SCOTT, and when her whistle blew the required passing signal, it would provide Captain Hemenger with an early warning of approaching traffic. It was a dandy plan with only one minor flaw: the brand new ISAAC M. SCOTT was running light, without cargo, while Captain Hemenger's boat had on just over 7000 tons of coal. Before long the SCOTT had pulled farther and farther ahead, her lights dimming into the fog. The sound of her whistle, continued and rang as clear as if she were tied up next to the GOODYEAR. Captain Hemenger had all of the pilothouse windows opened and stood propped on a side sill, listening intently.

Even in July Lake Superior's water was glacial as always as the GOODYEAR's steel hull pushed through it into the widening expanse of Whitefish Bay. The night's cooling of the hot humid air from the preceding July day had condensed the moisture into the fog that now hung around the boat. Captain Hemenger figured that by the time his vessel got out onto the open lake, where the air mass was less protected by the land and normally cooler, he would be out of the fog. Once in the clear he expected to ring Chief Gibson for more revolutions and make up some of the time the fog had cost him.

An oscillating brightness in the cotton fog became apparent to the left of the GOODYEAR, the Whitefish Point light. Apparently, as the boat neared Lake Superior the fog was opening a bit. Soon Captain Hemenger would turn to port and straighten on a Duluth course, and hopefully a short time thereafter would pass from the fog. As soon as the light was on the GOODYEAR's beam, Captain Hemenger would note the time and a memorized time-speed-distance result would tell him where to turn. At that time he would turn from the 330 degree course he was now steering to a 300 degree course that would take him to a point 12 or so miles off Manitou Island, when he would point the GOODYEAR on a 253 degree course until off Devils Island, then on a 240 course to Duluth. As the good captain picked up his pencil to note the time as 5:31 a.m., there came a rumble like distant thunder that coated the inside of the pilothouse. Then followed a distant groan, like tortured steel, accompanied by a series of deep-throated frantic whistle blows. The GOODYEAR's captain, wheelsman and thirdmate stood frozen like mannequins in the pilothouse. "What was that?" the watchman's muffled voice questioned into the fog from off the bridge wing. A moment later he cracked open the pilothouse door and stuck his head in. "What in blazes was that, did you hear that?" he questioned toward the motionless pilothouse crew. Batting his hand toward the puzzled watchman, Captain Hemenger shushed him, "Listen, listen, just listen," he whispered. Shouts could be heard through the distance. Reaching for the GOODYEAR's engine telegraph, Captain Hemenger rang "stop".

The whole darkness was shaken by an earthquake-like rumbling. To those on the GOODYEAR it seemed as if a freight train were passing in front of the pilothouse windows. A hollow silence followed, then more shouts and screams. Captain Hemenger threw the knife switch that set off the GOODYEAR's general alarm. He knew now that a giant lakeboat had just died out in the fog, and he would need all hands awake and on deck if his boat were to save any lives at all.

Every porthole on the GOODYEAR's hull suddenly illuminated. Lifejackets were snatched from their pegs and bare feet slapped in the condensation on the steel deck as a confused crew gathered in the night onboard the motionless oreboat. Down in the engine room Chief John Gibson came plowing in and took charge, ordering one of the frightened stokers to "...get up there and find out what in hell's kitchen is goin' on..." Word quickly spread among the rattled crew that there had been some sort of sinking and they were to watch for men in the water. Soon Captain Hemenger rang "slow", and navigating on the screams, the GOODYEAR began to creep toward the sounds of the disaster.

Through the fog the amber glow of a row of ship's lights became dimly visible. The odor of dirty steam, coal smoke and hot steel hung heavily in the air. Suddenly a series of quick blasts from the other boat's whistle shocked the silent crew hanging on the GOODYEAR's rail. Captain Hemenger blew in response and rang "stop" once again. "Lower the boats!" he shouted across the spar deck. Haste was in order—there were men in the water just off the GOODYEAR's bow. From the forward rail a life ring was flung and with that the rescue began.

One by one blue-lipped sailors were plucked from Lake Superior's frigid grip. The brilliant white beam of the GOODYEAR's spotlight probed the fog like a long white arm. A jumble of wooden wreckage, oil drums, life rings and splashing sailors were revealed. As soon as he assured himself that nothing living was in his path, the GOODYEAR's master inched the big freighter ahead once again. Carefully proceeding to the far side of the wreckage he came upon a wounded laker. With his crew in the yawls attending to the men in the water, Captain Hemenger turned his attention to the crippled vessel that remained on the surface. The spotlight darted about the vessel's bow revealing a massive hole, in fact the beam of light at one point shone directly through. Higher on the steamer's bow the beam illuminated her name...ISAAC M. SCOTT. Her maiden voyage had ended in a collision with another oreboat. Now she sat drifting, her bow gashed open to the inrushing lake.

Oblivious to the brand-new ISAAC M. SCOTT's proud passage at the Soo, the 436 foot JOHN B. COWLE had been at the same hour hauling eastward on a dead calm Lake Superior. In the COWLE's cargo hold was 7000 tons of red iron ore. Much like the ISAAC M. SCOTT, the COWLE was owned by one company, but operated by another. When she came out on November 1, 1902 she was the pride and joy of the newly-formed COWLE Transit Company. For the sake of profits, though, she was run by the massive United States Transportation Company. Tonight the boat's quiet routine under the command of Captain Wallace G. Rogers, continued to proceed normally as she approached Whitefish Point. The only thing abnormal had been the thickening patches of fog. At midnight Captain Rogers took his place in the pilothouse in preparation for bringing his boat down to the Soo. Upon taking charge, the captain quickly assured himself that the COWLE was on course for Whitefish Point. In spite of the splotches of fog, the United States Transportation Company would deliver its ore.

The SCOTT had just straightened out on course for Manitou, when ten minutes past the Whitefish Point light, the dark steel hull of the COWLE loomed broadside to him through the fog. There was no whistle blowing fog signals, no warning at all, only a few dim lights after it was too late. Grabbing the SCOTT's chadburn he rang for reverse and shouted "Hard left!, hard left!" It was a useless order. The laws of physics had sealed their fates. Before the SCOTT's big screw could stop in order to reverse, and her giant steel rudder could become effective, the SCOTT slammed into the COWLE, cutting her nearly in half. Some 15 feet of the SCOTT's bow penetrated the COWLE— Captain McArthur was nearly thrown over the big brass chadburn, on which he still had a grip.

For a long agonizing moment the SCOTT paused, bonded to the COWLE in a death embrace. The mate had blown the danger signal on the whistle as if his instinctive yanking on the whistle-pull could undo the nightmare. Captain McArthur dashed from the pilothouse to the bowrail. As with all lakeboat men, a glance up and down the other steamer told him what he had collided with. "It's the COWLE," he whispered into the confusion. A moment later, the SCOTT's engine found the reverse that Captain McArthur had ordered before the impact, and the boat shuddered astern. The grind of twisting steel shrieked through the mist as the SCOTT's bow pulled from the massive hole in the COWLE's beam. With a lurch, the COWLE listed and began to quickly founder. Captain McArthur bounded back into the pilot-house and slammed the engine telegraph to "stop". From the SCOTT's bow, a line was thrown to the deck of the sinking JOHN B. COWLE. As the SCOTT pulled away, three sailors desperately scrambled hand over hand onto the SCOTT. With the boat sinking beneath their feet, other sailors simply ran for the rail and leaped into the lake in an effort to get as far from the suction as possible. With a deafening roar the COWLE plunged beneath Lake Superior's icy depths, leaving behind only wreckage, the broken-nosed ISAAC M. SCOTT and those of her crew lucky enough not to have been pulled down with her. The passing of the COWLE took only three minutes.

By the time Captain Hemenger and the FRANK H. GOODYEAR arrived on the scene, Captain McArthur was functioning strictly on instinct. Shouting through his megaphone Captain Hemenger asked about the SCOTT's condition, and if the boat could make the Soo. From the SCOTT's spar deck her master shouted that he felt his boat would not sink, and that he thought they would make the Soo if the collision bulkhead held.

At daylight, it was obvious that anyone not aboard the SCOTT or the GOODYEAR was gone beneath the lake with the COWLE. The COWLE's master, Captain Rogers had survived in spite of having given his personal lifejacket to his son who had been aboard as a guest. The Captain was taken aboard the GOODYEAR which proceeded to Duluth. Tenderly, Captain McArthur nursed the SCOTT back to the Soo. His shiny new charge sported a massive hole in her bow, and her forward compartments were flooded. Many at the Soo expressed the belief that had the SCOTT been loaded, she would have joined the COWLE on Lake Superior's bottom.

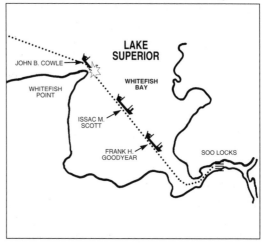

Over the months and years that followed, claims were filed, hearings held, voices raised and fingers pointed. Yet, nothing could change the fact that the JOHN B. COWLE and 14 of her crew were resting in the mud under Lake Superior. The COWLE, however is not alone in her grave. Just to her south rests the steamer VIENNA, an 1892 victim of a collision with the steamer NIPIGON. To the north the steamer JOHN M. OSBORNE, another collision casualty, had been waiting since 1884 for the COWLE's company. In later years, others would join the fleet in limbo below the surface of the Great Lakes, never to complete their trips.

The ISAAC M. SCOTT would last only four more seasons. Captain Archie McArthur and all of the boat's crew would subsequently be devoured by the "Great storm of 1913." It would take 63 years before the SCOTT would be found upside down on Lake Huron's bottom, her rudder bent and disabled. At this moment both the ISAAC M. SCOTT and JOHN B. COWLE rest mutely in the pitch black of the Great Lakes icewater museum, their sounds of disaster forever silenced.

Lost 'n Found . . . 'n Lost

*E*arly on a hostile Sunday, November 10, 1901, the logging tug TEMPLE EMERY was pounding along an aggravated Green Bay, just off Menominee, Michigan. Tagging behind the tug in the shape of a cartoon balloon came the raft of logs she was transporting. More than a million and a half board-feet of logs were contained in the raft, which stretched about a half mile wide. Such a moving of logs is an inexpensive mode that is used even today, and in 1901 these floats were commonplace. As morning passed into afternoon, Green Bay's mood went from foul to ferocious with a southerly storm wind quickly building. Stout sharp waves that the bay is well known for, began to assault the raft, and in short order the logs were churned apart into a helter-skelter of floating timber. Northward toward the beach went the wayward logs as the crew of the TEMPLE EMERY ran their tug for Menominee, to wait out the storm and muster enough man power to retrieve the timber when it made shore. Little did they, or anyone else on the lakes for that matter, know that the storm-tossed booms heaving on the surface of Green Bay were a precursor of things to come. This was the start of a five day rampage that would assault a number of different vessels and mariners around most of the lakes. If it were possible to hop into a time machine and look back across the years, this is how the week would unfold.

By Monday, both lakes Michigan and Huron were being agitated by the increasing November storm. Fall's nasty disposition has always been taken in stride by Great Lakes mariners and Monday's vessel traffic toiled along as usual. Of particular consequence were a number of vessels working on Lake Huron's Georgian Bay.

33

While the luckless TEMPLE EMERY was losing her raft, the lumber steamer MARY PRINGLE was beating her way across Georgian Bay. Bound for Tonawanda, New York with a deckload of rough-cut lumber, the steamer had the 176 foot schooner-barge SWEETHEART in tow. With her decks also stacked with lumber, the wooden SWEETHEART was in her 34th season of labor on the lakes. As the two boats approached the southern-most passage out of the bay at Tobermory Point, they ran head-on into November's temper. The weather could not have picked a worse time to fall apart. The waters off the point were already the grave site for nearly twenty wooden vessels.

Ice cold wind blowing across the relatively warmer water formed a radiation fog known as "sea smoke". That, along with blowing sleet, reduced visibility to less than a mile. Onboard the barge SWEETHEART, Captain Keller kept a sharp watch on the steamer through the spume. Through his binoculars he saw the PRINGLE suddenly jolt, and list. With that, the towing hawser went slack and the barge closed on a collision course with the steamer's heels. In an instant Captain Keller knew that the PRINGLE had found the shallows and his boat's own inertia was driving him into her. The resulting collision, in this storm, would probably doom both the PRINGLE and the SWEETHEART. In an act of pure desperation, Captain Keller ordered the wheel flung hard over, and waited for the barge to alter course.

With painful slowness, the barge's bow swung to starboard. Just as it looked as if the SWEETHEART would clear the steam-er, there was a low rumble as she too ran aground up alongside the PRINGLE. With a short vibration the SWEETHEART stopped, leaving only the shrieking wind to fill the air. The south wind held the two there side by side as the waves worked them over. When inspecting the SWEETHEART's hold, Captain Keller found startling evidence of the schooner's meeting with the shoal. A large boulder had crashed completely through the oak hull and was now lodged in her hold. As darkness fell, a slight shift in the wind allowed the PRINGLE to work herself free. Among the din of

The powerful "Rabbit Boat" D.F. ROSE is seen here in 1901 with the schooner-barges BOSCOBEL and MARINE CITY in tow. Later that year, the ROSE, pulling MARINE CITY along with the THOMAS HOLLAND and BAHAMA would be caught in the grip of a powerful gale that would spell the end for many wooden boats.

breaking seas, groaning lines and cursing sailors, the SWEET-HEART was brought free. Temporarily rigged together, the pair pushed onto open Lake Huron.

Bruised by the shoal and beaten by the storm, the PRINGLE was having a devil's time pulling the wounded SWEETHEART across billowing Lake Huron. A further concern was the giant boulder wedged in the barge's bottom. If the working of the boat's planking should loosen the big rock it would drop out, and the result would be like pulling a plug. To add to their plight, the over-the-bottom speed of the boats was now practically nil. More power would be needed to get the pair to a safe port. Through the fracas, like the answer to a prayer, came the lumber hooker ARMENIA. After a brief volley of megaphone shouts, a deal was made for the ARMENIA to aid the pair to the port of Alpena, Michigan nearly due west across the lake. By

Monday morning the trio had only made mid-lake and the storm had intensified to gale force. To add to the trouble, the ARMENIA's coal bunkers were running dangerously low. With little in the way of options at his disposal, the ARMENIA's master decided to call the deal off and cut the PRINGLE and SWEETHEART loose to find their own ends. As the ARMENIA sailed off, the PRINGLE and SWEETHEART were last seen wallowing in the rampaging seas, to be swallowed by a snow squall. A few hours later the ARMENIA hissed into Alpena, and her Captain wasted no time reporting the two lame boats he had been forced to leave behind in the gale.

The next day, Tuesday, back on Georgian Bay, others of the lumber fleet were heading into the storm. Steaming out of Blind River came the powerful 146 foot D. F. ROSE. Following behind the rabbit came her consort barges THOMAS HOLLAND, MARINE CITY, and finally the BAHAMA, all stacked high with pulpwood. While heading southward out of the north channel the four lumber-laden lakeboats faced a furious south gale. The sea fog mixed with snow blinded the way to Mississagi Strait and the string of boats was forced to feel its way using clock and compass. Then, much like the PRINGLE the day before, the ROSE found the rocky bottom of the bay. In short order, the whole flock was entangled on Scarecrow Island.

Some 43 miles to the east, northeast, the wooden lumber hooker PORTER CHAMBERLAIN was haulin' on the schooner-barge H. J. WEBB. At nearly the same moment as the ROSE and her consorts hit Scarecrow, the CHAMBERLAIN slammed into Darch Island with the WEBB following. Waves exploded over the stranded boats, and super-cooled spray encased everything in a brittle coating of ice. Thicker and thicker the snow became until the boats resembled icebergs. Amazingly, other passing boats could recognize the grounded vessels, and by mid-day the word of their plight reached Alpena. The tug RALPH departed into the storm for the D. F. ROSE, and at noon the tug JOHN OWEN fought her way toward the CHAMBERLAIN.

That same Tuesday, startled vessel watchers saw two ghost ships return from beyond. The PRINGLE and SWEETHEART, which the ARMENIA's master had reported as in great peril, steamed casually into the St. Clair River. Dock-side rumors had both vessels sunk in northern Lake Huron, but they hissed downbound and tied up for coal bunkers in Detroit. When the SWEETHEART's Captain was asked about the vessels' plight, he simply shrugged and stated flatly that his vessel was not in any danger at any time. As both boats sailed off for Tonawanda, the SWEETHEART still contained the boulder she had picked up in Georgian Bay.

Traffic on the Detroit River came to a halt when the storm reached its peak and the south winds gusted near 65 miles per hour, blowing the water out into Lake Huron. By midnight Tuesday the water level over Lime Kiln Crossing was measured at 16 feet nine inches. Dozens of lakeboats tied up at Detroit and Smith's coal dock. Still more dropped their hooks off bar point waiting for the gale to ease and the water level to rise. At Toledo, the cyclonic storm was blowing more from the west, and lowering the water. The Maumee River was down three feet, which the 298 foot wooden oreboat MECOSTA discovered when it became grounded outbound above the Cherry Street bridge.

The storm also was having its way up on Lake Superior and off Munising, Michigan it found a handy victim. Riding at anchor and hoping to wait out the weather was the 210 foot schooner-barge CONNELLY BROTHERS, with Captain William Keenan in command. The lake soon overpowered her hooks, and the five year old wooden boat was driven onto Sand Point four miles from Munising. The O. W. Blodgett steamer ZILLAH along with the tugs LAURA and HICKLER went to the barge's aid, but were unable to budge her in the storm. Finally the CONNELLY BROTHERS crew were removed, and left the boat with the waves breaking over her. They hoped that with a little luck and the barge's youth, she might not go to pieces.

With a great deal of hard work the tug RALPH freed the D. F. ROSE. Together they pulled the BAHAMA and MARINE CITY off the rocks. The HOLLAND remained stuck fast, her crew removed by the Thunder Bay Island lifesavers. Leaving the tug behind to work on the HOLLAND, the ROSE headed back down the lake. In a short time it became apparent that the MARINE CITY was more wounded by Scarecrow Island than first thought. In fact, she appeared about to go to pieces in the waves. With no little haste, her crew took to the yawl and were picked up by the ROSE. The derelict MARINE CITY was cut loose and left adrift on Lake Huron.

At Darch Island the tug OWEN had worked well into Wednesday evening, but had made no progress whatsoever in pulling the PORTER CHAMBERLAIN, or the WEBB off. Amid the pulling ropes, the howling wind and the pelting snow, the CHAMBERLAIN's pilothouse door burst open. A drenched Engineer, his hair frozen like straw, stumbled in gasping that there was a fire down in the engine room. By the time the captain and forward hands made their way aft across the ice-slicked deck, a large amount of smoke was billowing from the vents and doorways. From the door to the engine room, the companionway appeared as a tunnel of fire. Moments later as licks of flame began to shoot up around the CHAMBERLAIN's stack, the crew took to the boats. Alerted by the smoke, the tug OWEN pulled alongside and took men over the side on the same lines that had been used in the salvage attempt.

In a surprisingly brief time the CHAMBERLAIN's superstructure was a massive inferno, and even through the sub-zero wind the heat radiated to the point where the nearby H. J. WEBB's hull began to smoke. Simultaneously, airborne embers from the roaring CHAMBERLAIN fell upon the tender schooner-barge. Fanned by the gale-force wind, the hot spots sprouted into small fires faster than the scurrying crew could douse them. The scene must have been nightmare-like, with shouts into the storm's blackness and numb hands tossing water from wooden buckets.

Hand pumps squeaked and delivered a paltry stream of water that could do little to combat the advancing flames, and the barge's masts were alight like tall trees in a forest fire. Gingerly the tug OWEN pushed near the burning barge. Quickly her crew were taken off and the tug backed away. To keep from being ignited, the tug stood off a great distance, packed with the ship-wrecked sailors. Rolling in the blizzard, they watched as the PORTER CHAMBERLAIN and H. J. WEBB turned into two giant bonfires. The CHAMBERLAIN was valued at 10,000 dollars, and the WEBB at 8,000 dollars, the equivalent of less than 36 hours operating expense of a modern lakeboat. Unlike most boats in 1901, both of these boats were fire insured.

At Detroit the 170 foot lumber hooker OGEMAW landed with her consorts the schooner-barges SAVELAND and M. I. WILCOX. Downbound from Lake Superior's Bay Mills, the trio had been forced to delay at East Tawas, and coming around the thumb of Michigan they had received a considerable dusting. A short distance out of Tawas Bay the OGEMAW's master, Captain Martin O'Toole realized that leaving the protection of Tawas Point was not the best decision he had ever made. With his long tail of barges and decks stacked high with lumber, turning in the storm was out of the question. He had no choice other than to fight across Saginaw Bay, rounding Point aux Barques and running for Port Huron. The cargos of all the boats were systematically plundered by the waves. Captain O'Toole spent a sleepless trip to the St.Clair River, watching his deckload wash away. By the time the three vessels came off the lake at Port Huron, the only thing keeping the remainder of the cargo aboard was the fact that it was encased in ice.

Wednesday ended with one additional victim being swept off Lake Huron. Loaded with fragrant cedar from Alpena, the 147 foot rabbit boat EMERALD took water and was blown onto Point aux Barques. With the ice water waves washing over their boat and the fires in her boiler extinguished by the in-seeping water, the EMERALD's nine crew members were exposed to the biting cold. Through the long frozen night they shivered, waiting to die of hypothermia, or to drown when the lake beat their boat to pieces. At dawn the following day, the lifesavers from Port Austin showed up and removed the trembling crew.

By Thursday, up on Superior, under the shadow of the Keweenaw Peninsula, the tug SCHENCK was enjoying a windfall of opportunity. After releasing the CONNELLY BROTHERS, the big tug headed back for Marquette. On the way, 43 miles southeast of Stannard Rock, she came across the drifting whaleback Barge 127. The barge had been in tow of the 497 foot submarine decker JAMES J. HILL, both belonging to the Pittsburgh Steamship Company. Lake Superior was more than the steel towing hawser could stand, and the barge broke adrift. With the gale roaring, the steamer could not turn and pick up her consort. When the SCHENCK found Barge 127 it was just north of Grand Island and in danger of going aground. Putting a line aboard, the SCHENCK took the wayward whaleback with her to Marquette.

As the SCHENCK and her prize were steaming toward Marquette, the 460 foot steamer HARVARD and her consort the 458 foot steel barge JOHN SMEATON were being lashed by the storm. Like Barge 127, the lake overcame the towing hawser and set the barge adrift. By the time the SCHENCK and her stray reached Marquette, her captain was informed that the SMEATON had fetched up five miles northwest of Au Train, about 25 miles from where the CONNELLY BROTHERS had just been pulled off. The SCHENCK was ordered back to Au Train to assist in the SMEATON's recovery. With the tug BOSCOBEL in her wake, the SCHENCK departed Marquette, her captain rubbing his hands together in gleeful expectation. This would be a profitable week for the SCHENCK, a profitable week indeed.

On Lake Huron, forty miles north of Thunder Bay, the 228 foot lumber hooker INDIA came wallowing through the storm downbound for Goderich, Ontario. Across the angry water the INDIA spied a deserted vessel drifting with the wind. Thinking

they had come upon a vessel in distress, the INDIA angled in on
the derelict. As the steamer drew near it became clear that they
had come upon an abandoned schooner-barge. It was the
MARINE CITY, and would be quite a prize when the INDIA
brought her back to Goderich. Certainly her owner, L. B. Parker,
would at best pay a substantial recovery fee, at worst the hull
could be libeled for the INDIA's service. Maneuvering in the fray,
the INDIA managed to get a line aboard the barge. As the beams
of the two wooden boats crunched together, four of the INDIA's
crew scrambled aboard the MARINE CITY. A thick towing hawser
was made fast and with the four sailors aboard to handle towing,
the two lumber carriers pressed into the storm

The storm had not slacked off by Thursday night. The wind
shrieked from the northwest at a steady 40 miles per hour.
Temperatures plummeted into the teens, and everywhere around
the lakes, vessels waited for November to release the seas from
its evil spell. At Marquette 25 lakers sheltered, 30 were behind
Whitefish Point, and there was a report that nearly 100 were at
Sand Beach. As far east as Lake Ontario the storm was blowing,
but there had been plenty of warning and vessels were moored
snugly to the nearest dock.

Into the night the INDIA pulled the MARINE CITY toward
Goderich. The seas thrashing them from astern each vessel's
hull, complained without end. There wasn't a lamp alight aboard
the MARINE CITY, her complements having been pillaged by the
wild lake. The four crewmen had boarded in daylight and none
had thought to bring a lantern. As the boats tossed through the
sackcloth darkness and thick snow squalls, the only indication
that the INDIA had of the MARINE CITY's following was the
resistance on the towing hawser. Abruptly the towline went slack
and the MARINE CITY again drifted at the mercy of Lake Huron.
The INDIA turned her spotlight aft, but its beam reflected only
off the horizontally-blowing snow. There was no point in turning
the INDIA to attempt to recover the barge. With the MARINE
CITY being unlit there was the very real possibility of a collision,

if the INDIA could find the barge at all. The INDIA had no choice other than sailing on to Goderich, with the hope that the skeleton crew onboard the barge would drop her hooks and wait for the steamer to pick her up at daylight. On Friday morning the INDIA steamed into Goderich and anchored to wait out the storm.

Friday night saw the storm winds dying to a bluster and activity on the Great Lakes, over the weekend, picking up where it had left off nearly a week before. In many cases, this meant picking up the results of November's tantrum. On Green Bay the lumber tug TEMPLE EMERY supported by an army of some 200 lumbermen, gathered the logs of its scattered raft. Like the boats on the lakes, many of the logs had blown ashore—most to be recovered, some to be left there. Still others were washed away into the lake, never to be seen again. At Au Train the steel barge SMEATON was pulled from its perch by the BOSCOBEL with the SCHENCK by-standing only as a spectator. The barge THOMAS HOLLAND remained fetched up in Georgian Bay, but the EMERALD was pumped out, removed from the thumb and sailed the following season. When the INDIA steamed from Goderich in quest of the MARINE CITY she found only the choppy lake. Estimating the winds and seas, the INDIA's crew calculated that if the boat had dragged her hooks she would have been blown ashore about 12 miles south of Goderich. Arriving there, the INDIA found an empty beach. The MARINE CITY had been devoured by the black storm and had taken the four luckless salvage sailors with her. Never to be seen again, the MARINE CITY stands as one of the few vessels on the lakes to be lost—and found—and lost again.

A New Wardrobe
for Mrs. Russell

*U*nder the watchful eye of Mrs. E. G. Russell, wife of a Buffalo vesselman, and Mrs. E. H. Meyers, three young maidens were on a summer excursion to Duluth, Minnesota. It was August of 1912, a time when even a journey of a few hundred miles was an adventure.

This trip would take the ladies to the far northwest territories of the Great Lakes. Once north of Port Huron they would glide across the open expanse of Lake Huron on a floating steel island. The only contact that they would have with the outside world would be the passing of downbound boats. When land next appeared, it would be Detour Passage and the mouth of the St. Marys River. With great fascination they were to watch as the forested riverbank slid past, and then the industrial wonder of the locks at the Soo. They would get to see giant steel lakeboats raised or lowered 20 plus feet so that they might pass between Lakes Huron and Superior. The ladies would witness the colossal construction project that would one day be the Sabin and Davis locks. Leaving the Soo their trek would take the ladies once more across the vastness of an open lake. This time it would be the most grand of all the lakes—it would be Superior, as deep as 1000 feet and surrounded by wilderness. The western tip of Superior was to be their destination, the booming port of Duluth, an "emerald city" built around iron ore. Certainly, this was not simply a trip across the lakes, but an adventure west, an adventure of a lifetime.

For the journey up lakes, five first class passages aboard the oreboat JAMES GAYLEY belonging to the fleet of Captain John

Mitchell, had been arranged. All the way up, first class service is exactly what the five ladies had been treated to by the GAYLEY's crew. Each meal was served by jacketed porters and the three maids were always addressed as either Miss Russell, Miss Stone, or Miss White. An atmosphere of polished elegance was created by the GAYLEY's crew, adding greatly to the ladies' sense of adventure.

On the night of the 12th, Mrs. Russell had seen to the tucking in of the three young ladies, all of whom were bubbling with anticipation over tomorrow's arrival at Duluth. It seemed she had scarcely fallen asleep when a resounding rap at the cabin door shocked her back to consciousness. Assuming as much poise as possible, Mrs. Russell groped to open the door. Captain M. M. Stewart, the GAYLEY's master, stuck his face through the open doorway. "Wake everyone and come on deck, we're about to be run into by another boat," he ordered in a calm, gentle but terse voice. Moments later, clothed only in their night dresses, the five passengers groped barefooted and half awake up the companion way and onto the GAYLEY's spar deck. Everything seemed immersed in a surreal fog. Off to the starboard side, like a ghostly sea monster, loomed another giant oreboat. With night-marish steadiness and lights aglow, the steamer pushed directly toward the ladies. The fog was rent with the ear-splitting hoots of steam whistles as the deck rolled, throwing the ladies from their feet when the vessels collided. Shrieks of terror were drowned out by the thunder of twisting steel plates, cascades of inrushing lake water and bursting steam lines.

When the JAMES GAYLEY was launched at Cleveland's Globe Iron Works in 1902, she was the twin to the FRANK H. GOODYEAR constructed from the identical plans at Lorain that same year. Both boats measured 436 feet in length, 50 feet in beam and 28 feet in depth. The only difference between the sisters came when Mr. Goodyear added lavish guest accommodations to his namesake. Each boat went straight to work hauling ore and coal for John Mitchell. The GAYLEY had worked the long hauls for nearly a full decade without special notice or complaint.

Coal from the lower lakes, some 8,000 tons of it bound for Duluth, filled the GAYLEY's hold this August night—a hold which now contained the bow of another vessel and was rapidly filling with Lake Superior. The GAYLEY lurched violently to starboard as the boat that impacted her began to withdraw with a low groan. Getting to his feet, Captain Stewart got his first good look at the boat that had collided with his. It was so close he could read her nameboard. "RENSSELAER" was spelled out in block letters. Laggardly, with a grind, the opposing freighter pulled loose from the GAYLEY's beam and began to vanish into the fog. The GAYLEY creaked loudly and began to settle into a list to her wounded side. A giant gouge had been ripped into the oreboat's hull just aft of her fo'c'sle, and the lake was rushing in so fast that it resembled a waterfall. Captain Stewart knew by the feel of the 4,777 ton hull beneath his feet that the boat not only was sinking, but was in serious danger of rolling over and taking all hands with her.

Ore-laden and downbound for Cleveland, the RENSSELAER had been towing the steel barge GEORGE H. CORLISS that likewise had a belly full of red ore. Captain C. D. Secord was in command of the RENSSELAER as she pressed into the fog. The 474

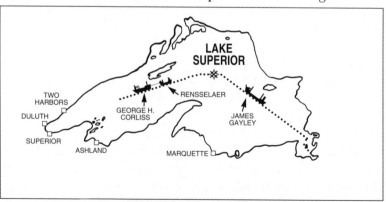

A New Wardrobe for Mrs. Russell

foot steamer came out in 1900, and her 378 foot consort started service eight years before. Both boats were now running for the massive Pittsburgh Steamship Company.

There is a chain of events that leads to any accident, but what locked this one into history was Captain Secord's consideration for the giant steel barge he was towing. In the back of his mind, the steamer's master knew that if he suddenly reduced the speed of his boat, the CORLISS would run right up his stern. As a result of this consideration, when he saw the GAYLEY's lights in the fog he could do little other than try to ease the RENSSELAER back. The towing hawser went slack and the CORLISS began to close on the RENSSELAER from behind, as she closed on the GAYLEY. Mass and the laws of physics did the rest. This is why the RENSSELAER appeared to close steadily on the GAYLEY. Finally Captain Secord could wait no longer and rang "reverse" on the engine telegraph and held on for what must come.

Colliding with the GAYLEY had severely damaged the RENS-SELAER's bow and all that was keeping her afloat was the integrity of her collision bulkhead—a delicate condition considering that ruptured boats filled with dense iron ore have been known to plunge to the bottom in minutes. Glancing over his boat, Captain Secord determined that he would stay afloat, at least for the moment. With this he made a quick and heroic decision. Ringing "slow ahead", he began to crawl back through the fog to the GAYLEY.

Returning to the JAMES GAYLEY, Captain Secord found the wounded oreboat in deplorable condition. Down by the head and listing to starboard, she appeared about to go under. In a maneuver of exemplary seamanship, he eased the RENSSELAER up along the perishing GAYLEY and nudged against her beam. Then using every rope they could muster, the sailors of both boats went to work lashing the two stricken vessels together. In a moment the three young maids were passed to the RENSSE-LAER. Before the others could be passed across, a series of

The nearly identical twin to the FRANK H. GOODYEAR, the JAMES GAYLEY worked for years in her sister ship's shadow.

sharp cracks echoed across the decks. The lines strung between the boats were parting as the two drifted apart. For a long minute those left aboard the sinking GAYLEY stood and watched as the RENSSELAER drifted farther away. Again the lifeboats began to lower and the GAYLEY's crew prepared to go over the side. Hooting the whistle the RENSSELAER again drew near the GAYLEY and hovered on her beam. This time there was no lashing of the two. The GAYLEY's people leaped for their lives at a point where the decks were about even. When the RENSSELAER's spotlight illuminated the last person leaving the GAYLEY, Captain Secord angled the RENSSELAER and the CORLISS away into the fog. Fearing the GAYLEY's red hot boilers might explode when the cold lake water reached them, he wanted to put some distance between his charge and the foundering GAYLEY. As the RENSSELAER was devoured by the fog, there came the ghastly roar of a succumbing giant. Alone in the mist, only 20 minutes after Mrs. Russell had awakened the ladies, the ore-boat JAMES GAYLEY took her final passage some 100 fathoms to the bottom of Lake Superior.

Onboard the RENSSELAER a crowd of castaways were milling about on the spar deck. Ominous low groans began to emanate from below decks, the boat moaning in pain from her shattered bow. Captain Secord, probing the forward areas with Captain Stewart at his hip, reassessed his evaluation of the RENSSELAER's seaworthiness. Both masters knew that if the bulkhead were to burst, the boat would plunge beneath them and join the GAYLEY in a matter of minutes. The order went out to begin blowing distress signals and to take up on the windlass in order to draw the barge CORLISS nearer. The ladies were then put aboard one of the RENSSELAER's lifeboats and transferred to the CORLISS, out of harm's way.

Just five miles off, the Richelieu and Ontario Navigation Company's 500 foot oreboat STADACONA heard the RENSSE-LAER's distress whistle. Moving slowly in the cottony mist the STADACONA attempted to home in on the distress calls. It took the better part of an hour for the boat to listen her way to the wreck scene. As she advanced toward the drifting RENSSELAER and her consort, a brief chorus of cheers rang into the night. Considering that the wreck had happened practically in the middle of Lake Superior, it was incredibly lucky that the STADA-CONA had been so near. The survivors easily could have sat drifting until the following morning.

As daylight broke through the fog, the five ladies were again westbound, but on their fourth oreboat in 12 hours. The STADA-CONA was now transporting them, along with the 20 other members of the GAYLEY's crew, toward Two Harbors, Minnesota. All of their possessions had gone down with the boat, and the refugees were left only with what they had been wearing at the time of the collision. Captain Secord and the RENSSELAER made a dash for Marquette, 95 miles south, arriving safely with the CORLISS still in tow.

Shortly after the STADACONA nuzzled up to dock at Two Harbors, a long rung ladder was lowered from the stern rail. With all the grace they could manage, the five ladies climbed down, clad only in their night dresses and the blankets they had been loaned aboard the RENSSELAER. Captain Stewart had the mate arrange for a carriage and accompany the passengers to a local hotel. Along the way, the mate spotted a ladies' clothier and had the driver stop. The shop keeper was a bit startled to see five ladies in night dresses, blankets and borrowed men's slippers shuffling through the door. "A new wardrobe for Mrs. Russell and the ladies..." the mate requested, "...Captain John Mitchell will see to the bill." On this trip, it is a safe bet that the five ladies had much more adventure than they bargained for.

Mate LeBoeuf's
Personal Disaster

*T*he first day of November, 1914 may not have been signifi-
cant for most people, but for John LeBoeuf it was a glad
day that brought back the worst of remembrance. This
was the day that the Dominion Wreck Commissioner of Canada
reinstated LeBoeuf's First Mate certificate. It had been two years
to the day since the commissioner had suspended the papers
and now LeBoeuf had his privileges back, just in time for the end
of one of the slowest shipping seasons in Great Lakes history. A
fitting way to wrap up the mess. LeBoeuf thought too of the "old
man", Captain Louis Daigneault, the master of vessels that Mate
LeBoeuf had served under and so often readily carried out
orders for. The commissioner had seen fit only to suspend his
master's certificate for one year. If this action was fitting—fair or
not—was an issue that LeBoeuf had turned over in his mind so
many times that the question just didn't matter any more. What
had happened two years before could not be undone, it was simply good to have it finally over. Regardless of the times or cir-
cumstances, LeBoeuf knew deep down that he alone was responsible for the ordeal. It had been a personal disaster of his own
making.

In Mate LeBoeuf's era the route between Lake Erie and Lake
Ontario consisted of a complex waterway designed to circumnav-
igate the rapids and falls on the Niagara River. The 27.6 mile
long Welland Canal greeted its first lakeboats in 1829 with a
series of 40 locks, all of which were needed to lower vessels the
320 odd feet from Lake Erie to Ontario, and raise them back
again. The original canal was rebuilt in a massive undertaking
between 1873 and 1887, reducing the number of locks to 25.

Typical in appearance to a series of canalers produced by the Swain Hunter Yard, the KEYSTORM was not around long enough to be widely photographed.
—Author's concept

Locks measured 270 feet in length by 45 feet in width and a very modest 14 feet in depth. During the same era, a series of locks of similar size were constructed and renovated on the St. Lawrence River, bypassing the Lachine Rapids. All of these locks created a route between the Great Lakes and the Atlantic Ocean, and they created a need for a special kind of lakeboat.

Steel steamers of less than 260 feet in length, and beams and depths to fit the canal locks, became a common sight along Great Lakes. A surprising number of these "canallers" were constructed across the Atlantic in the British Isles. These tiny steamers, with their pilothouses stacked on the bow and their engine accommodations located on the stern, were the seed for many a scoff from those who built salt water ships. Surely such a strange vessel could never pay its way on the high seas. After all, of what good use could such a small ship be, with that small cargo hold and so little draft? Yet one after another the strange dwarf lakeboats slid from the construction ways and sailed westward toward the St.Lawrence canal and the Great Lakes. It was there that the canallers worked efficiently and at a respectable profit.

By 1910 the canallers were becoming quite commonplace on the eastern Great Lakes and a rather familiar sight on the other lakes. One such commonplace canaller came down the ways at Swan, Hunter and Wigham Richardson Ltd. at Wallsend-on-Tyne England that same year. Launched as KEYSTORM, hull number 844 measured 258 feet in length, 42 feet across her deck and 20 feet in depth. Pounding her way across the Atlantic, the 1,037 ton KEYSTORM hopefully was on her way to a lucrative career for her owners, the Keystone Transportation Company. Once on fresh water, she joined her sister ships KEYWEST and KEYPORT scurrying about the lakes and seaway.

The KEYSTORM was in her second full season of canal service on October 25, 1912. She had been climbing the canal steps with clockwork efficiency, carrying just about everything from canned goods to grain. Most of the canaller's work was done on Lakes Ontario and Erie, and she crossed the U. S. Canadian border with great regularity. This day the canaller's hold was being filled with coal at the Charlotte, New York dock on the south shore of Lake Ontario. First Mate John LeBoeuf was sheltering himself from the late October nip just aft of the pilot-house, supervising the KEYSTORM's loading. As the seaway-bound coal began to top off the canaller's scanty cargo hold, her deck hands busied themselves in trimming the load. When the pile below the hatches peaked at 2,273 tons, LeBoeuf ordered the hatches covered and made his way into the pilothouse to advise the captain that the load was aboard and trimmed. Captain Louis Daigneault had been patiently sipping his coffee when the mate reported. The captain ordered the ladders pulled up and the lines let go and shortly thereafter the canaller hissed off for Montreal, Quebec. It was just after three o'clock Friday afternoon.

By four o'clock the KEYSTORM was making good black smoke four miles out on Lake Ontario. Captain Daigneault had given the pilothouse over to First Mate LeBoeuf for the run up the lake. Holding a 049 degree course on the compass would

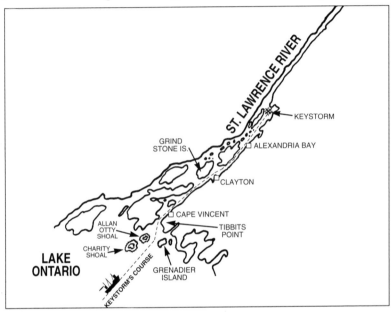

bring the KEYSTORM about three miles off Main Duck Island, in Lake Ontario's northeastern tip, in just over six hours. Unusual for late October, the lake was nearly flat calm and the captain had plenty of time for a leisurely dinner and some peaceful hours in his cabin.

Just before 10 P. M. Captain Daigneault returned to his pilothouse and brought the KEYSTORM just south of Main Duck Island. Now he had her course altered slightly, more to the north in order to keep Charity and Allan Otty shoals on his port side in just over an hour, and to enter the St. Lawrence River around midnight. At 15 minutes past midnight the canaller approached Tibbets point, and the mouth of the St. Lawrence. The captain checked her speed down to the normal eight miles per hour used for passing the river. Passing the town of Cape Vincent, the boat began to encounter small patches of the infamous St. Lawrence River fog. These blotches of fog are known to slam down like a thick wall of cotton, with little or no warning. Normally this encounter would have given a vessel master cause to check the vessel's speed again. Captain Daigneault did not.

Just before one o'clock Saturday morning Captain Daigneault casually turned charge of the KEYSTORM over to Mate LeBoeuf. Considering that his boat was running in developing fog, and in the narrow, island-studded, shoal-lined confines of the St. Lawrence, Captain Daigneault's action was far more than careless. The KEYSTORM was facing an unending stream of upbound vessels, some of which would simply materialize from out of the hanging mist. Even though Mate LeBoeuf was a fully and properly licensed officer, it was the captain's time to guide the boat. As the canaller passed abeam of Carleton Island, her master made his way to his quarters below the pilothouse and in a short while his cabin light went out.

Mate LeBoeuf's idle watch over the pilothouse began to grow tense as the KEYSTORM drew near Grindstone Island. Those scattered patches of fog were now turning into thick banks. At times he found himself guiding the boat into areas of near-zero visibility. By three o'clock that morning the KEYSTORM was abeam Alexandria Bay and running in near constant fog. As the boat approached Sister's Island light, the visibility opened up a bit and Mate LeBoeuf breathed a little easier. The canaller passed the light with no trouble and pressed on into the night. A moment later she was swallowed whole by a bank of dense fog. So thick was the muddledness that the boat's steering pole was difficult to see. The normal reaction of most navigators would be to watch the compass, or better yet to come to a stop. LeBoeuf, however, turned his attention to the aft pilothouse windows.

Over the stern, the mate was trying to steer by the diminishing glow of the Sister's Island light. It was his hope to hold his course that way until he could spot the gas buoy light on

Her career cut short, the KEYSTORM appears here in one of only two existing photos.

Chippewa Point shoal and perhaps move into the clear. His dilemma deepened as the light over his stern was steadily consumed by the mist. Now LeBoeuf began a frantic rustling of his charts and referrals to his compass. He had been steering the KEYSTORM for so long in lopsided reference to that light off the stern that he no longer knew just where he had the boat. Finally Mate LeBoeuf traded pride for panic and sent the watchman down to wake the captain.

The crewman had not made the bottom of the ladder when the whole boat lurched to her beam and began to grind to a rumbling, sudden stop. Captain Daigneault burst from his cabin and bounded up the ladder past the watchman, who was still trying to regain his balance. When he reached the tilting pilothouse he found the first mate standing there, his face as white as death, unable to speak. The KEYSTORM had run onto Scow Island Outer shoal, at nearly three quarters of her full speed. Shortly before four in the morning Captain Daigneault yanked the engine telegraph to "stop" and started the boat's whistle blowing the danger signal. When he contacted the engine room, he was told that the boat was taking water and that the pumps were being started. For a long time the captain and mate stood silently in the wheelhouse.The folly of their ways began to catch up with the KEYSTORM.

Morning came and the fog remained. The chief had kept the pumps running as long as possible but the disemboweled steamer was settling fast and soon they were overwhelmed. As the boat began to shift and groan the crew took to the lifeboats. With the rumble of a continuous earthquake the KEYSTORM slid off the shoal, just five hours after Mate LeBoeuf had guided her there. As the crew watched from a safe distance, there soon was nothing more than a boiling mass of wreckage as the boat left behind anything that would float and was not fastened down.

In less than a week after the KEYSTORM passed into the shipwreck charts, the Dominion Wreck Commissioner had completed his investigation. His finding was that Captain Daigneault "...showed a lack of judgement in allowing the mate to have charge of this valuable vessel in that particular locality, where there were still dangers to avoid when he went off watch, and in less than two hours it would have been daylight." The commissioner found that Mate LeBoeuf showed "...utter disregard of the compass course to be steered..." On Friday, November first, 1912—exactly one week after the KEYSTORM had left the Charlotte coal dock—the Wreck Commissioner suspended Captain Louis Daigneault's Master's papers for one year and mate John LeBoeuf's certificates for two years. Further, the commissioner gave credit to the boat's engineer for his efforts with the pumps in spite of the inrushing water. It was further suggested that "...a printed card of all courses and distances on the various runs should be hung in the pilothouse of all steamers for instant reference in cases where the leading lights or marks become obscured by fog or otherwise, as happened in this case."

As time passed the KEYSTORM's cargo was salvaged. Louis Daigneault's Master certificate was restored as was John LeBoeuf's First Mate certificate. Time pales even the greatest of disasters, and such was the case for John LeBoeuf and the woe that he carried with him during those two years. Today all of the players in Mate John LeBoeuf's personal disaster have long since passed on. Only the mute hulk of the sunken KEYSTORM remains as witness below the icy surface of the St. Lawrence. Pleasure boats, lakeboats and ocean ships pass her, unaware of her story and the two men who cut her profitable career short.

Gundersen's Island

*W*hen it comes to the spectrum of Great Lakes sailing in 1905, Captain Peter Kilty and Captain Louis Fredreksen were on opposite ends. Captain Kilty walked the steel decks of the big three year old car ferry PERE MARQUETTE 18, while Captain Fredreksen had the worn wooden decks of the schooner JOHN V. JONES beneath his feet. The car ferry earned its keep with year-round shuttling of railroad cars across Lake Michigan from Milwaukee, Wisconsin to Ludington, Michigan. On the other hand, the JONES was able to sail only when the lakes were clear of winter's ice and normally carried lumber products. It is likely that Captain Kilty barely gave a thought to the little schooner or its master, for it was just another of the flock of wind-powered freighters that the PERE MARQUETTE 18 had to give right-of-way to, whenever their paths crossed. Just before dawn on Saturday, October 21, 1905, both masters would meet under conditions that would be both tragic and welcome.

On Wednesday morning, October 18, the JONES was squatting at St. James on the upper tip of Beaver Island in northern Lake Michigan. Filling the hold of the 130-foot schooner and stacked upon her deck was nearly a quarter of a million board feet of fresh-cut hardwood destined for Milwaukee. The JONES was working toward the end of her 29th season on the Lakes, having slid down the ways at Manitowoc's Rand-Burger ship yard in 1876. Her career started out in the general merchandise trade, then shifted to coal and iron ore before the turn of the century. Recent years had seen the two-masted schooner's trade turned to lumber. Years of hard work and harsh weather had already taken their toll on her hull. The sharp edges of her planking had long ago been worn round, but her calking seemed always to hold.

Including Captain Fredreksen, the JONES worked with a crew of six. A Scandinavian immigrant, Captain Fredreksen felt that he got the best work of persons from the old country. Actually all but one of his crew were Scandinavian immigrants. The Captain's brother, Jacob, was charged with the duties of first mate, and sailors Hans M. Hansen, Olaf Gundersen and Ever Olfsen, worked the rigging like demons. Only cook William Thompson used the English language without a thick accent. For the most part, the cook felt like he was the one in a foreign land, what with all the Scandinavian conversation that filled his tiny galley. To the others, cook Thompson's ability to make a hot, 'stick-to-yer-ribs' meal in a single cook-pot made him one of their own instead of an immigrant in his own country. Life onboard a Great Lakes sailing vessel in 1905 was perpetually wet and cold, and that's just the way Captain Fredreksen's Scandinavian crew liked it.

As Wednesday morning turned into afternoon, the winds appeared favorable for the JONES's departure from Beaver Island. By four o'clock Captain Fredreksen had the schooner away from the dock and headed down Lake Michigan. With a fair bit of northeast autumn wind at her heels, the windgrabber appeared destined to make good time to Milwaukee. Rounding the south tip of Beaver Island, the boat had to turn nearly due west and thread the five and one half mile passage between Richard's Reef and North Fox Island. By nine o'clock the schooner was slicing through the passage in pitch darkness and an hour later Captain Fredreksen brought the schooner around onto 210 degree heading. With her bow pointed directly at Milwaukee and the wind up her sails, the JONES was going to earn a good day's pay haulin' down the lake.

One thing that can increase the profitability of any merchant vessel is a reduction in the time it takes to deliver its cargo. Such a saving could take place when a vessel loads more quickly, unloads more quickly or simply makes better time between ports. In the case of the JONES there was no real way to speed the loading or unloading of her cargos, but when the winds came up strong so did the schooner. A strong wind that might send steamers to shelter could save the JONES a full day in trip time. Every day saved might mean one more trip before the winter could end the season. At midnight the winds began to freshen, still on the schooner's heels, until by early Thursday morning they had mounted into a respectable storm. To Captain Fredreksen this was like money in the bank. If the winds held, the J. V. JONES would make her run to Milwaukee much more quickly and he would have plenty of time to scratch up another cargo. Through the night the schooner was definitely at her best, running ahead of a welcome storm.

The following morning cook William Thompson's breakfast had thoroughly satisfied the entire crew and preparations were underway for lunch. One thing that a schooner-born cook must be able to do is prepare meals in the worst of seas. By 10 a.m. the J. V. JONES had made short order of the last 160 miles, thanks to the same storm that kept the cook extra busy. At the boat's wheel, mate Jacob Fredreksen was reveling in the slashing wind, the rolling seas and the freshwater spray. The JONES was now about 17 miles off the Wisconsin shore and coming abeam of Sheboygan. About the same time as the mate began to feel snow pecking at the back of his neck, the winds began to suddenly die. The once full sails of the schooner rippled, then sat in irons for a long instant as the sailors scrambled to compensate. With unexpected violence, the storm exploded from the northwest. Captain Fredreksen shouted the orders to set storm sails, a task that the crew had already mustered to do.

Lake Michigan's seas began to break over the schooner, plucking away at her deck cargo, layer by layer. The JONES was now caught in a hard place with her head to a confused and growing sea and a gale force wind on her beam. Tilted in a sharp heel, her timbers groaned their familiar foul weather song. For

Captain Fredreksen there was no choice other than turning and running before the wind. By the time the JONES was rigged to fight the tempest, the winds had swung to west southwest. Now the schooner would have to tack against the winds in order to make Milwaukee.

Through the entire day Thursday, Captain Fredreksen zigzagged into the blow. Darkness came like a prowler and still the JONES fought on, but her progress toward Milwaukee was close to nil. By midnight the schooner's 29 year old hull began to show its age. Her response to the seas began to slow—each wave that slammed against her timbers worked her seams and calking without mercy. The groaning of her timbers took on a lower, more ominous tone. This could mean that the aged schooner's beams were parting, and that Lake Michigan's ice water was seeping into her hold.

In the pitch black of Friday morning October 20th the JONES's crew manned the schooner's pumps. Wind screamed over the boat as if sent from hell itself to take the schooner and its crew with it to a frigid doom. At nearly a mile a minute the snow came across the schooner, peppering her crew and cargo. The sailors worked her pumps in desperation, but their efforts were in vain, for the J. V. JONES had already become waterlogged.

About three o'clock in the morning, with the waves like hills of black ice and the snow shooting horizontally, the JONES listed one final time and agonizingly rolled onto her beam. The roar of shifting cargo drowned out the shouts of the shipwrecked sailors as the schooner capsized. What remained of her deck cargo cascaded into the churning sea, the lumber lifted by the lake and sent crashing back upon the JONES and her helpless crew. Clinging to the overturned hull, they were pummeled by the waves, laced with the sharp-edged hardwood cargo. To add to their plight, there was a heaving mass of deck workings and gear that had been swept from the JONES when she went over.

Each wave took more than its toll in bruises and pain as it crashed over the men. The cold served up a like share of agony as well. Within the first half hour hands and feet were numb, and the wind stung noses and ears like a swarm of angry insects. The shock of the schooner's turning turtle was nearly as stinging to the crew as the cold itself. Throughout the night they clung to what once had been their home and was now just a bobbing hulk.

As the black of the deadly night began to turn to the light of dawn, a passing steamer appeared on the fitful horizon. With painful slowness the oreboat drew near, trailing a long smudge of coal smoke behind. In chorus, every one of the JONES's imperilled crew began to scream and wave their frozen arms and hands. With a belch of smoke from her stack, the steamer seemed almost atop the castaways. Then with nightmarish steadiness it pushed past them and toward the horizon. By mid-morning another vessel was sighted in the storm, barely visible between the rolling waves. Once more the shouts and waves came from the shipwrecked sailors. Again they went unseen. They were just too low to be spotted among the billowing seas.

By late afternoon, Captain Fredreksen could see that his people were in a bad way. Their hands growing too numb to grip the hull, all were clinging with their elbows and knees. Occasionally one would shout to another, or a head would raise to face the unyielding storm and gaze toward the tossing horizon. Captain Fredreksen noticed that cook William Thompson was not moving and crewman Ever Olfsen had not moved in a long while. Before long the lake washed the two lifeless bodies from their frail grip on the JONES's timbers and swept them into the tangle of wreckage about the boat's bulwarks. There they remained as if wanting, even in death, not to be separated from their suffering shipmates. The bodies became a constant reminder of the numb fate that might be ahead for all of the schooner's crew.

The skies grew dark with evening, as the storm blew on with a frozen rage that seemed without end. In the hours before nightfall more freighters had appeared and slipped away, but the storm-beaten sailors were now too weak to wave or shout. All were just too weary to let Lake Michigan tease them any more. Deep in his being Captain Fredreksen knew that none of the JONES's crew would see dawn if they remained dipped in the lake. Shortly after dark there came a rumble like a distant battle ship firing a salvo. The schooner's hull shifted in an odd way and those clinging to her thought that she was breaking up. Woeful minutes passed but the schooner did not come apart. Late in the evening there was another rumble, then a third, and with that the hull began to roll, dumping everyone into the lake. Thrashing about in the wild lake, their frantic cries were those of men facing the end.

Shortly after midnight, the Pere Marquette Steamship Company's 358 foot steel car ferry PERE MARQUETTE 18 pulled clear of her slip under the portly command of Captain Peter Kilty. The distance from the slip to the Ludington outer breakwater was less than a mile and without doubt Captain Kilty's presence alone would have gotten her that far. He was a rock of a man, with a belly to match his boat and an ability to command that matched his grizzly bear hands. His boat was able to smash its way across Lake Michigan's frozen surface in February's worst, so this little October blow was hardly more than a bother to her giant captain. As one o'clock Saturday morning approached, the PERE MARQUETTE 18 swung southwest on a 226 degree heading for Milwaukee. Her head to the storm, the seas began to burst over her high bluff bow, throwing spray completely over her pilothouse. Captain Kilty's boat pounded on, as if not to notice the pest-like waves.

Far to the west on Lake Michigan the JONES's men were still fighting for what remained of their lives. Somehow Olaf Gundersen managed to surface and paw his way onto something large, solid and floating. Wiping his eyes clear with his sopping wet sleeve, he could see that he had fumbled aboard the now up-righted hulk of the JONES. On elbows and knees he made his way forward, half crawling and half swimming across the swamped deck. Avoiding the maelstrom of wreckage, Gundersen found the fo'c'sle and made his way atop it. There he found himself, if not high and dry, at least elevated a good five feet above the sting of the bitter lake. Soon both the Fredreksen men as well as Hans Hansen had gathered atop Gundersen's island, huddling to find shelter from the wind. Looking aft, they could clearly see why the JONES had rolled back onto an even keel. Her foremast and main truck had been snapped off by the action of the storm and it was the spars that had apparently been hold-ing her over. The stays of the foremast were still fastened tightly to the boat and it simply sloshed at her beam like a big telegraph pole. With her deckload gone, the cargo of hardwood sealed in her hold buoyed the wreck up, and the J. V. JONES became the world's biggest liferaft.

When the first brightening of Saturday morning began, the PERE MARQUETTE 18 was still rock-solid on course for Milwaukee. The weather had let up a bit and now Lake Michigan was a rude chop below a low gray sky. Just 35 miles northeast of port, Captain Kilty's ever-cautious scan of the lake around him caught a glimpse of an object among the fitful seas. Putting his binoculars to his eyes made the object tossing in the dis-tance become more pronounced but not more clear. Instinctively,

Wreckage strewn, the JOHN V. JONES arrives at Jones Island, Milwaukee. Sunk to her rails, only the hardwood cargo trapped in her hold keeps the wreck afloat.

he sensed mariners in distress and ordered his boat turned toward the object. Soon the big steamer started to come upon boards of hardwood scattered by the storm. At half past seven in the morning the big car ferry eased up near the wallowing wreck of the JONES. The sight was a sad one, for everywhere there was heaving wreckage. Surrounding the wreck was an abundance of tangled sails, ropes, casks, hardwood—and two floating bodies. Four other motionless figures were positioned, as if cowering, atop the fo'c'sle. Scanning the wreck with his binoculars, Captain Kilty saw that he had come upon the tragic end of a once proud schooner. He could not help but think of the horror of those four men—apparently frozen atop her prow.

As the giant car ferry gingerly eased closer to the derelict in order to positively identify her, one of the figures on the fo'c'sle lifted its head, then another stirred. Instantly Captain Kilty realized that the men on the wreck were alive. They were simply so beaten by the cold and wind and so near death that they had been oblivious to the steamer's arrival. With that, the captain yanked the car ferry's whistle pull and a series of blasts snorted from the steamer's funnel. All four of the figures stirred and the order was given to lower the car ferry's lifeboats. With the PERE MARQUETTE 18's steel hull breaking what remained of the wind, her boats shuttled the JONES's four survivors from a frozen death. In a semi-conscious state they were taken into the steamer's toasty cabins and brought back to their senses.

At noon the PERE MARQUETTE 18 backed to her slip at Milwaukee and discharged her load of railroad cars. Disembarking was the crew of the JONES, including the bodies of William Thompson and Ever Olfsen. The four survivors recovered to sail again and the hulk of the JONES was salvaged, towed to Jones Island at Milwaukee and returned to service. She sailed on for nearly a decade more in the lumber trade, until the decline of the industry led to her discard.

Captain Kilty received a meek wave of thanks from Captain Fredreksen as the schooner master limped from the PERE MARQUETTE 18. Returning to the pilothouse, the car ferry's master peered out toward the lake. Today had been a good day for him, for he had beaten that lake out of four helpless souls. But Lake Michigan would have its revenge on Captain Kilty and the PERE MARQUETTE 18. On September 9, 1910 the car ferry would spring an unexplained leak and plunge to the bottom, taking him and 22 others with it. Ironically, the car ferry rests today at nearly the same place where the lake overwhelmed the JONES five years before.

Chief Gibson's Post

*C*aptain Russell Hemenger stood over the washbasin peering toward its edge in a hollow stare. His mind was blank, yet at the same time it was a smear of simultaneous thoughts. With events rushing beyond his grasp, Captain Hemenger felt the instinct to pull himself together. "Shaving", he thought, yes—doing something normal would help, "shaving would be good". His hand trembled almost uncontrollably when the foam was brushed to his cheek. As he opened the straight razor, there was a commotion at the cabin door. A second later the door burst open and a swarm of tight-vested newspaper reporters sporting derby hats hovered over Captain Hemenger. He did not hear their questions. He simply stared toward his image in the mirror, wishing the horror would leave his memory. "How could it have happened?" he asked himself over and over and over again. And what of his good friend John Gibson, what could have possessed him? And there were the images of Lillian and John Bassett, images Captain Hemenger would take to his grave. The reporters continued like vultures, picking away for a quote or some tidbit of fact. He wanted to order them off the boat, but this was not his boat. Captain Hemenger's boat was on Lake Huron's bottom with her back broken. Now he was but a guest onboard the steamer JAMES B. WOOD.—a powerless witness to a disaster that, although beyond his control, he still felt responsible for.

Forty eight hours before the press burst onto Captain Hemenger's sorrow, he stood command in the pilothouse of the Mitchell and Company's 436 foot oreboat FRANK H. GOODYEAR. It was just before dinner on the 22nd day of May, 1910 and the GOODYEAR was pushing downbound on a 145 degree heading into Lake Huron. The evening was shaping up to be pleasant, at least for the time being. Captain Hemenger, like everyone else who made their living on and around the Great Lakes, knew that spring was as unpredictable as fall, and a pleasant sunset could easily lead to a troublesome night.

Strolling aft to the galley, Captain Hemenger cast a discerning gaze over his boat, which was in truth a thing of grace. When she first found fresh water at Mitchell and Company's Lorain shipyard in 1902, she was the pinnacle of the shipbuilder's toil. Her length was optimum for her power and her profile was identical to her sister ship the JAMES GAYLEY. The GOODYEAR however, bore the name of her owner, transportation magnate Frank H. Goodyear. Being so named, it was only fitting that Mr. Goodyear should fit his namesake with special accommodations to tend to his comfort when he was aboard. For this the tycoon had plucked from his Buffalo and Susquehanna railroad his pet passenger car number 110. The car was permanently affixed to the center of the boat's spar deck, where it became both owner and guest quarters, insuring that the GOODYEAR's namesake and his cronies would always travel in a manner to which they were accustomed. By 1910, Frank H. Goodyear had been dead for some three years, but Captain Hemenger's command still sported car number 110 and Mr. Goodyear's name.

Approaching the stern, Captain Hemenger entered the domain of Chief Engineer John Gibson. It is said that although the captain may command, the boat really belongs to the chief, and such was the case aboard the GOODYEAR. Captain Hemenger ruled as king from the pilothouse, but deep in the boat's engine room, Chief Gibson reigned as duke of all that made the boat function. In fact there were many cases, such as fuel bunkering and maintenance lay-ups, where Captain Hemenger would take his directions from Chief Gibson. At the moment, the careworn captain's orders were coming from the sandman and his empty stomach. A hot meal and a few well-deserved hours of sleep would end his workday.

In the galley, cook Frank Bassett was serving up another of his filling suppers. Nearby, his mother Emma was busy with the clean-up and his wife Lillian was pitching in, while at the same time tending to their three year old son John. Instances of whole families serving in the galley of an oreboat were not uncommon in 1910. A good cook was an invaluable asset that many a vessel owner would go to great lengths to keep. After all, a well-fed sailor works longer, harder and in worse weather, with fewer complaints. Considering that a sailing season on the lakes keeps a cook away from home from April to December, if signing his kinfolk keeps him happy, no problem.

An hour out of Detour, the FRANK H. GOODYEAR was plowing southward into a charcoal Lake Huron night. As per the captain's orders, and supervised by First Mate Gus Zaetsch, Wheelsman Jacob Plergis held the oreboat on a 145 degree heading until about an hour before midnight, when she was to settle in on the 157 degree heading that would take her to Port Huron. Just after four a.m., Captain Hemenger returned to his pilothouse and relieved Second Mate Archie Fullon who had short-shifted the First Mate. At the same time John Pappa took the wheel and William Pitt took the watch from William Schluter. A cold mist hung all around the boat, and a thick accumulation of condensation had gathered on the wooden sill of the open pilothouse window. It was fact that the captain took respectable note of as he ran his finger through it. The year 1910 was, after all, long before N.O.A.A. satellites existed to picture shifting weather patterns in advance. All that Captain Hemenger had to work with were his instincts and experience. The rapidly-decreasing visibility outside the pilothouse windows foretold what might be a slumbering spring storm, to hit perhaps within the next day. Possibly the GOODYEAR could make Port Huron before the weather fell apart.

Shortly before dawn, cook Frank Bassett rang the first bell for breakfast. Down in the GOODYEAR's engine room Chief Gibson was getting an early start with his beloved machinery.

The chief's days normally started very early, with the boat's workings requiring his close attention. Often the slightest quiver or vibration would transmit through the boat's structure and wake him like an alarm clock. As he began this morning of picking over every detail left from the previous watch, his belly asked for the first meal of the day. Oilers Howard Shook and William Row were passing the can and chatting briefly about the oiling schedule as their shifts changed. When the second bell rang from the galley, Chief Gibson was considering sending Fireman Ernest Streek up to bring him something back, as it was on his way anyhow. This way the chief wouldn't have to leave his engine to waste time on a meal.

Nearly all of the off-duty crew had responded to the second bell and the galley was quite full. Wolfing down a heap of food before taking his shift stoking the GOODYEAR's boilers, was Polish immigrant Standersiaw "Stosh" Kiubokweski, his job demanding that he fuel himself before fueling the fires. Sliding up to the GOODYEAR's big wooden galley table came Deckhands Louis Kramer, Iver Carter, Fred Herman and Frank Jankovits, as well as Second Engineer George Grant and Fireman Frank McIllick. Thick breakfast aromas curled about the GOODYEAR's stern. Suddenly, ear-splitting blasts from the boat's whistle splintered the breakfast clamor. The feasting galley occupants froze for a heartbeat or two, some with forkfuls of food poised just short of their open mouths. An instant later the galley lurched and rolled, tossing nearly everything to the tilting floor. Dishware rained smashing to the deck, and the giant cookstove pot flung its boiling water into the confusion. A thundering rumble, as if a freight train were crossing the spardeck, drowned out the chaos.

Below, in the GOODYEAR's engine room, Chief Gibson was attempting to get back to his feet. Hindered by the still-tilting deck and a jumbled mass of tools, coal and other debris that had scattered about him, the chief was having a tough time getting up. Steam hissed and filled the room and all around was the

The pride of her owner, Mr. Frank H. Goodyear, the steamer bore his name as well as his favored railroad car as owner's quarters (visible midship). In 1910 she took both to the bottom of Lake Huron with her.

sound of suffering hull plating. John Gibson's domain had suddenly become a dark steam-filled abyss. The chief knew instantly what had happened—a collision—and the GOODYEAR had taken it on her beam. His first instinct was to do everything in his personal power to save his boat.

Up on deck the scene was a mixture of confusion and terror. Crew clamored toward their lifeboat stations, others struggled toward their quarters in a hurried attempt to save their possessions; all grabbed their life-belts. Through the clouds of escaping steam, the dim outline of the boat that had collided with the GOODYEAR could be seen. Hovering, stunned, only a few yards off the GOODYEAR was the 534 foot oreboat JAMES B. WOOD. With little warning in either pilothouse, both boats had suddenly appeared to one another through the dense pre-dawn fog. Before anyone could take action to change their fate, the WOOD had slammed into the GOODYEAR's beam at nearly full speed. Upon impact the WOOD's bow had sliced deeply into the GOODYEAR's hull and she sat as if in shock, with Lake Huron inundating her hold full of iron ore.

It was immediately clear to everyone on the GOODYEAR that their boat was mortally wounded. Deep steel-toned groans and distant hollow bangs began to fill the night as jets of air shot through the gaps between the hatch planks. The GOODYEAR's crew could sense the hull moving beneath their feet in a strange and unthinkable manner. This movement signaled that she would soon slide away beneath them. Atop the GOODYEAR's after quarters, frantic hands were attempting to launch the lifeboats. Some of the crew simply leaped over the side in an attempt to get clear of the foundering boat. One of these was Emma Bassett, who'd been tending to galley chores when the whistles of both boats drew her out on deck. She witnessed the two slam together and thought the GOODYEAR was going over right then and there. She stumbled to her cabin and dug for her lifejacket. It was as if she were stuck in the slow motion of a nightmare, as she fumbled in panic for her life belt and ran for the rail. In her haste, she could just get the life preserver over one arm before she leaped toward Lake Huron's frigid water.

Captain Hemenger noticed that Chief Gibson was conspicuously absent from the crowd. The chief was standing at the GOODYEAR's engine controls waiting for orders to be rung from the pilothouse. Waiting perhaps for the "ahead full" ring in an effort to beach the boat, or for any order that he could implement, as if he could keep the boat afloat through his own resolve alone. Captain Hemenger dispatched Engineer George Grant to the companionway door leading to the engine room. "On deck at once, John..." the engineer shouted into the steam. There came only a muffled response. "This boat's in no condition to be beached...the boat's leaking fast!" the crewman urged.

Whether the GOODYEAR's back broke, or her bulkheads burst or both is really academic. What is important is that the boat plunged to Lake Huron's bottom so swiftly that those atop her decks abruptly found themselves being pulled beneath the lake, trapped in the big freighter's vortex. Onboard the WOOD her crew had scrambled to the rails and then stood there in shock. Their eyes were riveted on the hill of wreckage boiling up from where the GOODYEAR had just been. The WOOD's whistle had just begun blowing distress signals and her crew were in mid-dash toward the lifeboats to aid the GOODYEAR's crew, when the steamer plunged. Among the churning jumble surfaced Lillian Bassett, clutching her baby son John. A moment later one of the heavy oak hatch planks shot through the surface endwise and crashed down upon the mother and child. They were not seen again.

Emma Bassett had found herself pulled beneath the water when the GOODYEAR went down, and clawed her way toward the surface. When she again found air, the boat was gone and all around her wreckage was popping to the surface. In the distance she saw someone clinging to a hatch plank, but before she could call out, she was pulled beneath the lake. When she surfaced the second time, Emma saw that the man on the plank was her son Frank. She began to shout, but no one heard. Emma felt herself growing weak, sapped by the icy water and the shock of the accident. She grew near to unconsciousness. Floundering in the wreckage, she came upon a piece of the GOODYEAR's deckhouse and gripped a windowsill. Floating there, too weak to swim, she shouted to Frank, asking about his wife and son. Through haggard cries he told her that he feared they had gone down with the GOODYEAR. Emma began to slip into unconsciousness. In all, the GOODYEAR took 19 people to a watery grave. It had been less than 25 minutes from the time Frank Bassett rang the second bell until his family had been claimed by the wreck of the GOODYEAR.

One half hour after the wreck, the WOOD's lifeboats began rowing through the maelstrom of floating wreckage. Plucked from the icewater were Captain Hemenger, Engineer George Grant, Fireman Frank Mollic and Frank and Emma Bassett. As the rescue effort expanded, the morning fog grew more dense. It was a strange setting for a disaster, as shouts from the WOOD's crew echoed through the mist and were followed by long silences. The lifeboats probed on, waiting for responses to the echoed calls—responses that would never come.

Captain Gibson, the WOOD's master, was busy making a survey of the damage caused by the collision. Having come out of the West Bay City Shipyard in 1906 the 534 foot WOOD was practically a new boat. Inspection of her bow showed her forward compartments flooding, but her collision bulkhead appeared to be holding. Apparently the builders in West Bay City had done some of their best work on hull 616, and that morning in the middle of fog-locked Lake Huron, their skill seemed to be paying off. The WOOD's captain took a gamble and decided to stay on the scene searching for survivors until the fog lifted. Considering that in its wounded state it would take more than 24 hours for the WOOD to limp to Port Huron, this was a gamble indeed. It was his bet that the pumps could keep the pressure off the bulkheads long enough to find any remaining survivors, and still make the St.Clair River.

For the next seven hours the JAMES B. WOOD squatted in the pea-soup fog, when around noon the layer lifted. Other than the WOOD's own life boats, there was no activity in sight. The WOOD's captain had waited on the scene far too long for survivors who would never be found. It was now time to leave, to get up steam and make for port. Her bow stove in, the boat could make only about four miles per hour in headway, and the 120 mile slog to Port Huron took 30 sorrowful hours. It was just past six o'clock Tuesday evening when the WOOD pushed her battered hull up to the Grand Trunk dock in Port Huron. Agents of the Gilchrist Line, the WOOD's management, were immediately notified of their boat's crisis.

In the coming weeks, months and years there would be flurries of legal documents, decisions and settlements regarding the collision. In time, all of this would fade away and the wreck of the FRANK H. GOODYEAR would rest on Lake Huron's silty bottom, nearly forgotten. The JAMES B. WOOD would be repaired and sail on in a long, profitable career, ending her days in Interlake colors as ARCTURUS. She was sold to overseas ship brokers, but foundered enroute in 1961.

Today giant modern self-unloaders pass directly over a point 19 miles east, northeast of Oscoda, Michigan on their way to Stoneport and Alpena. It is doubtful that modern sailors, or summertime pleasure boaters for that matter, give any thought to the tragedy that unfolded there in 1910, or the wreck that rests below. Perhaps only Great Lakes historians keep the memory alive, but that is what they do best. Only research scuba divers with advanced equipment may visit the decks of the FRANK H. GOODYEAR 200 feet below Lake Huron's surface. To those who pass overhead and those who explore her hull, a word of warning—Chief John Gibson is still at his post, tending to his beloved machinery as he has since 1910. Although others may come and go, the GOODYEAR belongs to Chief Gibson.

Hoodoos, Mistaken Identities
and a Captain's Tale

*L*ike most Great Lakes vesselmen of his day Captain Frank Patterson had his share of superstition, but he was much too busy managing the affairs of the J. C. Gilchrist Company's 210 foot wooden schooner-barge W. S. CROSTHWAITE to let such things occupy too much of his time. In fact when the worn oars on the boat's yawl were replaced with second-hand oars from the company's steamer WAVERLY, which sank shortly thereafter, he really did not give it a second thought. When the CROSTHWAITE's yawl itself was replaced with the discarded yawl from the Gilchrist steamer SITKA which went to pieces on Lake Superior, Captain Patterson pondered the coincidence, but did not lose any sleep over it. However—when he discovered that the mate had hired on a deck hand who was off the schooner-barge F. B. GARDENER that had burned on Lake Huron only weeks before, the idea of a "hoodoo" began to haunt him.

It was a fairly routine day at the Soo, routine for late autumn that is. The sky hung low and gray and it appeared the bases of the fast-moving clouds would collide with the treetops. This time of the year the sailors put on as many articles of clothing as they could comfortably wear, attempting to gain insulation through a layering effect. In 1904, oilskins or thick woolen coats were used as a shield against the elements. On this blustery day a bitter wind bit at the skin and ran a deep chill through the body, regardless of what you were wearing. As Captain Charles Garey brought the 160 foot wooden steamer WYOMING around Big Point downbound for the locks, his pilothouse clock read just after two o'clock in the afternoon and the usual traffic jam of vessels wasn't there. Slowly but steadily he lined the boat up in the long channel. Just short of the fork, he slid her over to the north wall. Easing her beam up along the pier he brought the vessel to a halt. Shortly thereafter the upper gates of the original Poe lock swung slowly open and the Cleveland Cliffs Iron Company's 380 foot steel steamer CENTURION began to slowly churn out. Meanwhile, in the adjacent Weitzel lock, Canada Steamship Lines canaller TADOUSSAC was being lifted to the Lake Superior level. It was Thursday, the tenth day of November, 1904.

Things at the Soo were vastly different in 1904 than they are today. Modern oreboats slip into one of four giant locks while crowds of tourists with clicking cameras hang over the rails of one of three observation platforms. In the fourth year of the 1900s there were no gift shops, restaurants, museums or other tourist attractions. Portage Avenue was instead crowded with the facilities for servicing the Great Lakes maritime industry. There was a Soo Locks Park, but no fences along the waterfront. The 1904 boat watcher could walk right up to the lock wall. Most prominent, however, was the difference in locks. Only two existed, the 515 foot by 80 foot Weitzel lock was where the MacArthur lock is today. The original Poe lock which measured 800 feet by 100 feet, operated where the current Poe now exists. Locking of multiple vessels in each lock was common, the two locks having been designed with multiple locking in mind.

When the CENTURION cleared, the WYOMING's engineer Charles Little got the "ahead slow" order on the engine room telegraph from Captain Garey. Like a snail, the boat pushed toward the lock. The WYOMING's profile was somewhat different from her Great Lakes kin. The traditional lakeboat had her pilot-house, officers and deck crew quarters forward, engine works and engine crew aft, with a clear deck in between. Although the WYOMING had a standard lumber hooker's hull, she had her pilothouse planted aft atop her stern quarters just ahead of the funnel. This "all accommodations aft" arrangement gave her more the look of a rabbit boat than the standard oreboat. Fitting—when you consider that her owners kept her busy in upper lakes lumber trade where rabbit boats were common. This trip was no different from most, the WYOMING's deck stacked high with lumber just the way her owner, Captain Garey, wanted it.

As the WYOMING slowed to stop once more and made her lines fast to the bits, the 370 foot steel package freighter MUNCY hissed into the lock behind her and tightened her lines as well. In good time, the two were lowered to the Lake Huron level. The lower gates opened just before half past three in the afternoon and the two lakeboats pushed clear of the lock. Waiting at the pier to take the WYOMING and MUNCY's place was the wooden laker VOLUNTEER and the 436 foot steel steamer J. C. GILCHRIST. As the WYOMING passed, the two upbound vessels were already letting go of their lines. Approaching the locks and rounding the bend upbound ahead of the WYOMING came the steamer A. D. THOMPSON towing her whaleback consort. Captain Garey pulled the WYOMING's whistle pull and snorted the first of many passing signals to be sounded before the boat reached Lake Huron.

At about the same time as the WYOMING was departing the locks, the 400 foot Gilchrist steamer E. N. SAUNDERS was lining up on De Tour Passage, preparing for the trip up the St. Marys River to the Soo. Trailing faithfully behind the steel oreboat was her consort, the wooden schooner-barge W. S. CROSTHWAITE and Captain Patterson—with a hoodoo on his mind. Although his boat was in its 31st season, one could barely tell by looking at her. Captain Patterson watched over the old boat as if he owned her himself. Her paint was always fresh, her sails were always tightly wrapped when not in use and her lines were always neatly coiled. Before the start of this trip Captain Patterson had seen fit to have her spar deck re-tarred in anticipation of November's temper and the snowbound winter lay-up.

This Thursday afternoon, another schooner-barge was moving into another river far to the south of De Tour. Interestingly,

Seen here loaded to the hilt, the tiny, powerful steamer WYOMING goes about her business. She, along with her owner and captain, Charles Garey, had been doing exactly that in the fall of 1904 when the end came.

this boat also bore the name CROSTHWAITE, WILLIAM CROSTHWAITE, under the command of Captain O. W. Thompson. This CROSTHWAITE was inbound on the Saginaw River with 410,000 feet of Ashland, Wisconsin lumber for the A. C. White Company of Saginaw, Michigan. There was always an inordinate amount of confusion between the two boats named CROSTHWAITE. They were nearly identical in appearance, and often the various ship reporting points would publish the passing vessel simply as "CROSTHWAITE". At one time, both vessels had been the property of Saginaw River vesselman William Crosthwaite, and the boat that sported his name was now headed into the Saginaw River, while the boat that was currently being towed toward the Soo was named for Mr. Crosthwaite's son. It was confusing.

Pointing the WYOMING's wooden bow down the St. Marys River, Captain Garey was about to pass down a river that, like the locks above, was considerably different from modern times.

The modern boat watcher can stand upon the banks of the St. Marys and feel lucky to see a half dozen lakeboats pass between dawn and dusk. In 1904 the WYOMING was met by a flotilla of Great Lakes maritime history. Below Six Mile Point she passed the OCEANICA followed by the FRANK W. HART and WILLIAM E. REIS. At Nine Mile Point came the CHOCTAW and an hour later the CHARLES R. VAN HISE pulling her consort barge BRYN MAWR. In rapid succession Captain Garey's boat encountered the JOHN J. ALBRIGHT, H. B. HAWGOOD, SCRANTON, CITY OF TRAVERSE and LAFAYETTE with her barge MAIA. This roll-call of classic lake boats would keep the modern day tourist's camera in high gear and make today's boat-nut jump with glee. To Captain Garey they were just passing signals to be sounded and maneuvers to be made. Through the darkness came the familiar lights of another steamer, the E. N. SAUNDERS and her barge W. S. CROSTHWAITE.

The time was just before eight o'clock in the evening as Captain Garey's hand reached slowly toward the whistle pull. Steadily the vessels moved toward one another, then, just above Rocky Point, the WYOMING's whistle let off two long blasts, the signal for a port-to-port pass. Long moments went by when all that could be heard was the wind playing with the rigging. Suddenly, the SAUNDERS reply echoed. The big steel steamer appeared to grow larger and larger ahead of the comparatively tiny WYOMING. Just when it appeared as if the SAUNDERS would blot out the shoreline, the two vessels silently passed each other. As the steamer's stern thrashed past the WYOMING's beam, the barge caught Captain Garey's eye. He did a quick double take and stepped close to the pilot house window. Slightly confused, he watched as the schooner-barge W. S. CROSTHWAITE drew closer and closer. He suddenly realized what he had been squinting at. All at once he turned to wheelsman Archie Richmond. "I thought for a moment that she was my CROSTHWAITE," he said with a chuckle, "and she's supposed to be in Saginaw 'bout now". Captain Garey not only owned the

WYOMING, but his Shannon and Garey company owned her schooner-barge kin WILLIAM CROSTHWAITE.

At quarter past eight, just above Twin Island and with the SAUNDERS and her barge shrinking astern, the WYOMING came upon the steel steamer AUSTRALIA and her ever-present consort AMAZON. In the 20 plus miles that remained of the St. Marys River, Captain Garey had yet another flotilla to deal with. Onward came the FRANK H. PEAVY, the EMPIRE CITY, CORSICA and their whaleback barges, THOMAS ADAMS, J. L. WEEKS, WILLIAM LIVINGSTON and lastly the whaleback steamer JOHN B. TREVOR and her whaleback consort. Since she left the lock the WYOMING had blown passing signals 21 times and passed 28 lakeboats in eight hours. Considering the traffic jam that would be gathering at the Soo tonight, Captain Garey was feeling relieved that he was on the open lake and not going back up the river. He handed the pilothouse over to mate John Devaney and and made his way to his cabin.

A traffic jam was just what the E. N. SAUNDERS and her consort W. S. CROSTHWAITE found when they arrived at the Soo shortly before one o'clock in the morning. Going up the Weitzel was the CITY OF TRAVERSE, and entering the Poe was the LAFAYETTE with her consort MAIA. There were eight boats coming up behind the SAUNDERS and three rounding Big Point to come down. The SAUNDERS had no time to waste and her master figured that if he dropped the CROSTHWAITE he could get up the Weitzel on the turn around. Considering both boats would together only fit the Poe and currently the two tin stackers were only just squeezing into that lock, the SAUNDERS left the W. S. CROSTHWAITE at the wall and moved for the Weitzel. After being lifted to the Lake Superior level the SAUNDERS's master tied her up in the upper channel and ordered up a tug to bring up the CROSTHWAITE. As go the best laid plans, it was five A. M. before the 683 ton barge could be brought up. This fact was dutifully noted by the ship-reporter, "upbound at 5; WILLIAM CROSTHWAITE." She had been confused with her cousin again.

In less than a half hour, the W. S. CROSTHWAITE and her towing steamer E. N. SAUNDERS were reconnected and haulin' up the St. Marys River once again. By eight o'clock Friday morning the pair cleared the river and pounded onto Whitefish Bay. Leaving the shelter of the river, the master of the SAUNDERS found a nasty amount of weather blowing. So foul was the bay that an hour out of the river, it was decided that the two boats wanted no part of Lake Superior. Shortly after noon the SAUNDERS hugged up close to Whitefish Point where the barge dropped her hooks. Immediately after letting the barge go, the SAUNDERS anchored. The two boats joined a growing fleet of sheltered vessels behind the point, waiting on the weather.

At that same hour the WYOMING was beating her way southward on a disagreeable Lake Huron, just off Thunder Bay. The winds were still stiff and bitter cold, with a nasty bit of chop running. Miss Addie Potter, ship's cook, was busy cleaning up after the crew had downed one of her savory lunches. Keeping her company were some of the crew, Joseph Witman, Stephen and Louis Nadeau and purser John Durosia. The other members—Archie Richmond, John Perry, Lynn Smith and William Whalen, the second engineer, were about the boat performing their duties. With the exception of the purser, who was from Sault Saint Marie, the entire crew was from Saginaw. The atmosphere around the boat was very light, despite the weather. After all, she was Saginaw bound. There she would unload and pick up the barge WILLIAM CROSTHWAITE.

By six o'clock Friday evening, out on Whitefish Bay, the atmosphere onboard the W. S. CROSTHWAITE was quite similar to that of the WYOMING. In the fo'c'sle the chore of laundry washing had been started. A large pot of water had been placed on the forward stove to heat, and the entire crew of seven was gathered aft in the galley for dinner. While the crew was feasting, the unattended stove began to heat the surrounding woodwork. Before long the structure reached the point of combustion and the walls were in flames. Swiftly the flames infected the forward areas, unnoticed by anyone. As the fire consumed the doors and the window frames, it got a taste of the freshly tarred and oiled deck. To say that this added fuel to the flame would be an understatement at the very least. Shortly the entire spardeck was afire. A single member of the crew stepped from the galley into what appeared to be a bright, hot summer sunset. The only problem was that this was November and the sun had gone down nearly two hours before. Peeking around the corner, the startled sailor's face was lit by the inferno on deck. In a heartbeat he dashed back into the galley and destroyed the light-hearted dinner atmosphere. "We're on fire!" he screamed.

The crew sat motionless for a moment. The sailor's ashen face, wide eyes and gasping breath shocked them all. Their shock turned into terror as they clamored through the door to fight the "fire". A single glance told them in a collective instant that the W. S. CROSTHWAITE was finished. Flames were leaping from the entire spar deck and the masts were engulfed. The bow was totally involved and there was no chance of fighting the fire. A strong southwest wind had blown the smoke over the side— that had kept the crew in the galley from smelling the blaze.

Everyone realized that the W. S. CROSTHWAITE was a lost cause and that they all were in immediate danger of burning up with her. Captain Patterson did not have to give the order, as some of the crew were already swinging out the yawl. Minutes later the whole bunch were gathered aboard and began lowering. About the time the falls began to squeak, Captain Patterson remembered that he had left 200 dollars in his cabin. Leaping from the yawl, he made his way toward his cabin door, but was driven back by the flames, already beginning to consume the aft deck house. A moment later the captain bounded back into the yawl and they lowered away.

Using the oars from the WAVERLY to row the yawl from the SITKA the crew of the W. S. CROSTHWAITE, including the refugee from the GARDENER, escaped the burning schooner-barge. The flaming boat lit the way across the stormy bay to the nearby E. N. SAUNDERS, and by the time the yawl arrived, the burning CROSTHWAITE had drawn the attention of every boat anchored on Whitefish Bay. One by one the W. S. CROSTH-WAITE's crew climbed the ladder to board the SAUNDERS. On deck, they watched for more than an hour as the barge was consumed to the waterline. The next morning the SAUNDERS returned to the Soo and Captain Patterson reported the boat's demise to the Gilchrist authorities. He told of his hoodoo, but nobody paid that much attention. When the word went out around the Soo that the schooner CROSTHWAITE had burned, the news services quickly put the story out naming, of course, the WILLIAM CROSTHWAITE as the lost vessel.

While the W. S. CROSTHWAITE burned on Whitefish Bay the WYOMING was some 25 miles above Michigan's thumb, still working down Lake Huron. At eight that evening the wind freshened from the southwest and began to blow at gale force. Waves began to board the little wooden steamer and pluck at her cargo. Luckily the WYOMING had a large steam engine, one of the largest for her class, in fact. The boat simply kept plowing ahead, slamming into the seas as she had done so many times before. Not long after the seas began to assault her, Second Engineer Whalen came slogging into the pilothouse, looking wetter and dirtier than usual. He wasted not a word in telling Captain Garey that the boat was taking on water. The captain ordered the syphons started, but was informed that Chief Engineer Little had been running the pumps for some time and the water was gaining. Chief Little had sent the second up to ask the captain to seek some shelter and give him time to pump out.

The only shelter near the WYOMING that would protect from a southwest gale was just off the tip of the thumb near Grindstone City. This is where Captain Garey pulled the WYOMING up as close as he dared to the shore, and found a bit of the lee of land. In the relative protection of the shoreline the boat could be pumped out without the lake molesting her hull. Captain Garey's current position was far from a secure one. With his boat tossing just off the boulder-strewn shore, Burnt Cabin shoal above him and the point below, he would be in a hard place if and when the storm winds shifted.

It took the better part of an hour for the pumps to catch up to and overcome the intruding lake. To Captain Garey it seemed much longer, as he stood in the WYOMING's tiny pilothouse keeping an ear and an eye to the weather. At length, the second engineer returned to the pilothouse and informed the captain that the syphons had gotten the water out of her. With that the wooden steamer was brought about and headed due north. The plan was to sail up about nine miles and round Point aux Barques in deep water. The WYOMING would then haul southwest down Saginaw Bay, head to the storm. It would be 64 nasty miles to the shelter of the Saginaw River.

Meager progress had been made before Chief Little (once more) saw the water rising in the bilges and below the floor grating. Again the pumps were started, but this time as Captain Garey maneuvered for shelter, the WYOMING started to waterlog. As it was clear that the steamer was in a bad way, the captain decided to turn and run for the beach. Down in the engine room, the normal heat and steam was being stitched with an unusual acrid stench. Investigation found a large amount of smoke coming from the wood framing surrounding the boat's giant boilers. As Chief Little fanned his hand to clear his view, stiletto orange flames suddenly licked out at him. The ferocious hunger of the rapidly-spreading flames caught the engineer off guard and he stumbled backward in spite of himself. An instant later the shock wore off and reality settled in—the WYOMING was not only sinking, she was on fire as well.

Again the second engineer flung open the pilothouse door. This time, the expression on his face said more than any garbled speaking tube or bell signal could. He started the boat's whistle blowing to alert the crew. Most of the crew were already involved in the pumping operations, but the few who were not, mustered in the engine room. As the bad water was being pumped out, the good water was being squirted on the flames. This little contradiction in logic did not last long, for soon the flames climbed the uptake and burst through the roof. Shortly, the heat drove the crew from the firehold and the pumps. Now the fire fighting had to be conducted from on deck.

When the flames were first discovered it was one half hour past midnight. In less than an hour and a half the situation had become hopeless. Flames were shooting out around the stack and bursting from every window. Luckily, the WYOMING's yawl was atop her deck cargo just forward of her aft spar, and was protected from the blaze. No sooner had Captain Garey given the order to swing the yawl over the side than the WYOMING rumbled from deep within. The fire had consumed the wooden structure that housed and supported her boilers. Now the cylindrical iron monsters were free to roll about among the inferno. A single roll of the hull and the boilers shifted to port, almost as if to turn the boat turtle. What remained of her deck cargo cascaded over the side in a lumber avalanche. Now the WYOMING was sitting dejectedly on the gale-swept lake, listing in a sinking condition, surrounded by floating lumber—with her superstructure in flames.

It was two o'clock Saturday morning when the WYOMING's crew took to the yawl and went over the side. The danger now was that the southwest gale would grab the yawl and carry it onto the open lake. If that should happen, by the time they blew ashore 90 miles later on the Bruce Peninsula, they would be just 12 ice-encased corpses. With this in mind the yawl was skulled only as far as the WYOMING's forward mast. To the mast clung Captain Garey and his crew, as the steamer continued to sink and burn. Lake Huron threw sprays of icewater over them without mercy, and the roaring wind brought temperatures near zero. In the lee of the wreck the crew shivered, the boat now completely on her side and settling fast. The end of the mast they clung to was only four feet out of the water.

Those bright, towering orange flames had been better than sending up a flare when it came to alerting help. The Port Austin life savers had seen the fire and knew immediately what was happening out on the lake. They launched their surfboat and pulled through the storm toward the fire on the lake. When the lifesavers at last arrived at the WYOMING, the settling boat had sunk to the point where the lake had smothered the flames. The crew clung to all that remained above the water, one foot of her forward mast. Quickly the lifesavers took charge of the survivors and the bunch pulled for the thumb. So high was the storm that it quickly became apparent that there was no chance of rowing back to Port Austin. They turned instead for Point aux Barques and made landfall safe and sound.

Monday morning Captain Garey and crew arrived in Bay City by train. Later that day, he met with Captain Thompson of the WILLIAM CROSTHWAITE which had finished her Saginaw unloading and moved to Bay City to wait for the WYOMING. After a brief discussion, it was decided that the WILLIAM CROSTHWAITE would lay up for the winter where she was. Her trip with the WYOMING was to be her last of the season anyway. The following day Captain Thompson exchanged two pennies for a copy of the Bay City Tribune, as the paperboy made his rounds along the docks. Scanning through the pages he came upon a headline that caught his eye, "SCHOONER BURNS TO WATER'S EDGE", it stated dramatically. Upon reading the next line, he was shocked to discover that the lost schooner was the one he was sitting on right now. "WILLIAM CROSTHWAITE, from Bay City to Ashland, destroyed by fire Sunday night," the kicker exclaimed. His boat had been mistaken for her kin once again— only this was to be the final time.

Captain Garey remained in the lakeboat business for many years after the WYOMING burned and sank. Coincidentally, he purchased interest in another lumber carrier, the MIAMI, and was her master for many profitable seasons. After the WYOMING had been sitting forgotten on Lake Huron's bottom for nearly 20 years, Captain Garey found himself again in command of a yawl as it rowed away from another burning steamer, this time the

MIAMI. As the MIAMI's lifeboat pulled across a glass-calm Lake Huron on that hot, hazy August afternoon with no shore or rescue in sight, Captain Garey occupied the crew with the tale of the old WYOMING and that bitter cold November night off Michigan's thumb. Doubtless as the story went on, the MIAMI's shipwrecked sailors felt a little bit better about their current plight.

A Deal's a Deal

*B*uffalo, New York took its first shipment of coal in the year 1842, the result of coal baron Guilford R. Wilson moving his operation from Elmira to take better advantage of the lake routes west. What kind of vision inspires men such as Mr. Guilford to seek out an untried opportunity by gambling on all of their livelihood can never be explained. In Mr. Guilford's era a businessman simply "rolled high," and won or lost. Guilford coal was initially hauled west by empty grain boats. Unloading their west-grown cargos of wheat, flax, barley and other assorted yields at Buffalo's elevators, the boats carried the coal out as simple ballast. Being the keen businessman that he was, Mr. Guilford let the coal go out for free, a sample, an appetizer to tempt the hungry western cities. It started slowly and by 1844 only 2,500 tons of Guilford coal had gone west, but by then the black fuel rocks were moving for hire. As the years passed the shipments grew as did the success of Mr. Guilford and, inspired by this, other coal-handling firms sprang up and joined in the profits.

By the first decade of the 1900s the tonnage of coal flowing from the Buffalo harbor numbered in the hundreds of thousands. At the Rochester & Pittsburgh Coal & Iron Company, for example, the loading process was both rapid and fascinating. A shoebox-like railroad car filled with coal would be ramped up to a dumper, displacing the previously-emptied car as the full car was locked in place. The entire car would be rolled over, dumping its cargo into a Receiving Pan. The pan was in turn emptied into two "Y" shaped buckets with trap-door bottoms. These buckets were hoisted from the dock and out over the boat's waiting hold, where the trap doors were opened, dropping the coal. More than 450 tons per hour could be dispatched in this manner. Steamers both wooden and steel sailed down with ore, grain or lumber and returned upbound with cargos of profitable Buffalo coal. Sailing vessels would make their way to the port specifically to fill their holds with the burnable stones, then wait days for a favorable wind to fill their sails.

October 1907 was drawing to a close, and the bitter brisk wind that whipped past Captain William Trudo's ears foretold of the coming of November. Clopping along the Buffalo coaldock's wooden walkway, he could see the low sky growing dark, and gray. There was not a lot of time remaining in the season of navigation. As usual, Captain Trudo intended to make the best of every day that remained. Being both the owner and master of the three-masted schooner ANGUS SMITH, he had to be not only a skilled navigator but a shrewd businessman and wheeler-dealer. A vessel such as the 188 foot SMITH could be a real money maker if it were properly managed and Captain Trudo was a master of every angle, be it in business or navigation.

Tonight the schooner had taken on 1200 tons of coal bound to C. M. Clute of Bay City, Michigan. The problem for Captain Trudo now was that the winds had been holding from the west for the last several days, which would not favor the boat's sails as propulsion. Considering that Mr. Clute was waiting for the coal far to the northwest with a strongbox of cash, Captain Trudo needed to improvise. Marching about the docks, it had not taken the enterprising captain long to find a steamer headed his way. Tied to one of the giant wooden docks hissed the 295 foot wooden steamer CHARLES A. EDDY. Her master, Captain McDonald, was making preparations for the trip up-lakes. A brief rail-to-dock negotiation took place between the two captains and ended with Captain Trudo pulling a large roll of money from his pocket and peeling away enough to close the deal. It was an arrangement that would allow the ANGUS SMITH to deliver her cargo against the winds, with enough efficiency to still come away with a tidy profit. Cash up front for a tow as far as the mouth of Saginaw Bay was the contract, signed of course with a handshake.

Sailing vessels such as the ANGUS SMITH could be quite speedy in the delivery of their cargos, given a favorable wind. In some cases, wind grabbers could top speeds in excess of 20 miles per hour, far faster than any steamer. With a crew of only seven to nine to feed and pay, a single schooner was a very lucrative portable business. So, as the EDDY steamed into position to pick up the ANGUS SMITH's bow on her towing hawser, the steamer's expense was just another item in the cost of running Captain Trudo's business. With a series of small jerks, the pair began to move toward the expanse of Lake Erie.

Buffalo's lights were still visible off the SMITH's stern, when the west wind began to freshen. The wind from this direction built waves from as far as Toledo and sent them rolling the length of the lake to confront the two lakeboats. Lake Erie is the shallowest of the freshwater seas and her waves are known for being sharp and coming in rapid succession. Tonight was no exception for soon the schooner-barge's bow began to pound against the whitecaps. Each impacting roller transmitted its energy to the SMITH's prow and was in turn transmitted along the towing hawser. As the EDDY pulled on, the seas began to break solid over her bow rail. The SMITH too was being boarded, and in a short while, her decks were continually awash. Before long the wind was screaming through the rigging of the steamer's three tall masts, as well as those of the ANGUS SMITH. The pair's over-the-bottom speed against the storm had slowed to effectively nothing.

Peering through his lead-glass cabin window, Captain Trudo was shielded from the sleet, but not from the consequences of the blow. Knowing that his passage through the storm was in the hands of Captain McDonald and the EDDY, Captain Trudo could but look into the blackness and wait. Daylight revealed the EDDY and the SMITH had hauled far less than the distance run in fair weather. Sloshing just off Long Point, with the storm intensifying, the two boats were receiving a considerable dusting. Now, as if the earth had tilted, the deck of the ANGUS SMITH rolled steeply, tossing everything and everyone about the deck. Moments later the deck rolled in the opposite direction indicating that the schooner-barge was blowing around into the sea trough. The message was clear to Captain Trudo. The towing hawser had parted, and the ANGUS SMITH was adrift in the seas.

By the time the SMITH's crew mustered atop the schooner-barge's wildly-heaving fo'c'sle, Captain McDonald had brought the EDDY in a wide arc, positioning her stern advantageously for a reconnecting. Showers of frigid water cascaded over the shivering deck crew as they struggled to re-rig the tow line. Frozen swear words swirled with the wind, but the job got done. By the time everyone's hands and feet were sufficiently numb, the EDDY was again hauling on the SMITH's bow. But no sooner had the frost-bitten crew gathered around the galley coffee pot, than the schooner's beam again rolled with the seas. The towing hawser had parted once more, forcing the already drenched sailors back out onto the sloshing deck. It took far longer to reconnect the line this time, for the storm was building in strength and the waves were breaking more solidly over the two boats. No sooner had the slack come out of the hawser than it parted. Apparently the old rope had rotted to the point where it could no longer stand the stress of heavy weather.

Captain McDonald once more drew the EDDY up near the ANGUS SMITH. He fought his way atop the steamer's pilothouse with the boat's giant megaphone in hand. Over the screeching wind he shouted to Captain Trudo that the EDDY would make for the port of Erie to pick up a new towline. The SMITH would be left on her own in the middle of Lake Erie's rage. Captain Trudo prepared to hold out as long as possible while the CHARLES A. EDDY pounded off into the fray. A steamer leaving a barge amid a blow was nothing unusual on the lakes. Actually, in these days of the tow-barge, it was an accepted and common practice. Many times the loosened barge was to fare better than the steamer, prime examples being the L. R. DOTY in 1898 and the MATAAFA in 1905. In both cases the barges rode out the winds and waves with only scratches. The MATAAFA slammed into the piers at Duluth and broke her back, while the DOTY just sailed away and disappeared forever into Lake Michigan. It was hoped that the CHARLES A. EDDY would return and recover the ANGUS SMITH from Lake Erie's grip.

The first task for Captain Trudo was to stabilize the ANGUS SMITH in the rolling seas. To do this he ordered both of the schooner's massive anchors dropped. The process required picking up each anchor with a deck-mounted hoist and dropping it over the side. It was a soaking, heavy-handed task in the face of the storm, but both hooks reached the lake's sandy bottom and in short order the SMITH began to come about and weather-vane into the seas. Gingerly, the anchor chain was paid out to reduce the stress and prevent parting. At 120 fathoms Captain Trudo called for the pins, the hooks took a firm hold and the ANGUS SMITH faced off against the gale.

Almost immediately, the rollers began to break completely over the schooner. The SMITH's taxed planking creaked in protest as it found itself between the lake and the 1200 ton pile of coal heaped in her belly. As daylight faded, the storm's temper heated further, and now the waves boarded the schooner's fore-peak and rolled solid across her full length. This was the time when Captain Trudo's tender loving care, of the schooner paid off for under the assault of the sea the ANGUS SMITH's butts held. Barely a drop of water leaked through her seams and hatches. It appeared that the boat would last the night. Attempting to remain as dry and warm as possible, the crew had gathered in the after cabin, expecting a sleepless night. Without warning, there came a ripping crash—as if a giant tree had come crashing down upon the deck. Captain Trudo grabbed the mate and the two of them forced their way through the aft cabin door. Showered by the cresting seas, they climbed atop the deckhouse. From that vantage point they could see that the schooner's forward mast had been up rooted and smashed down upon the deck. Cascades of water were swirling through the gaping hole where the mast had once been planted.

While the captain and mate pondered the damage from what they thought to be the safety of the deckhouse roof, an enormous sea broke green over the bow and rolled directly at them. In an instant the two were swallowed by the icewater hill and swept toward the lake. Out of blind instinct, Captain Trudo clawed toward anything that might stop his slide toward death. With luck, he managed to tangle among the aft stays and held there until the wave expended itself. Clearing his vision, he got himself upright and looked about for the mate. To Captain Trudo's relief he found the mate also tangled in the stays, like a bug in a web.

By the time the two shaken sailors climbed down from the roof, they found that the giant rogue wave had twisted the deckhouse from its foundation, and subsequent swell was taking advantage of the twisted structure. Water shot in from the deck, flooding the cabins below. Everything from the ship's stores to the crew's possessions turned into a sloshing flotsam. Manning the hand pumps, the crew did what they could, but as the night wore on it appeared that the lake was getting the better of the ANGUS SMITH.

Through the storm-racked night, the Lehigh Valley Transportation Company's 400 foot steel package freighter WILKESBARRE had steamed toward Buffalo. With the seas at her heels the steamer was taking a wash over her stern, but was making good time. Between the blowing spume and raining sleet, the WILKESBARRE's forward visibility had been reduced to nearly zero and she'd been forced to navigate across Lake Erie on clock and compass alone. By morning the storm began to calm nearly as fast as it had blown up, and the WILKESBARRE was now sailing into a fairly moderate chop mixed with a thick sea-smoke.

At mid-afternoon the WILKESBARRE's pilothouse watch caught a glimpse of two tall masts jutting above the fog. As the steamer drew near the wounded schooner, it was evident that they had come upon a vessel that had taken the worst of Lake Erie's anger. Ahead of the steamer wallowed the ANGUS SMITH, now drifting with what remained of the storm's breeze. Apparently, during the night, the lake had seen fit to relieve the schooner of her anchors. A glance at the SMITH revealed that the boat was not in immediate danger of foundering, but was in considerable need of a tow. As Captain Trudo made his way to the rail to hail the WILKESBARRE, he had no inkling that his problems had merely started with the storm.

As the WILKESBARRE eased alongside the SMITH, the masters engaged in a brief negotiation. The deal was made from megaphone to megaphone and was for the Buffalo-bound steamer to take the SMITH with her, for a fee, of course. There was no handshake this time to close the deal, but the SMITH's bow was attached to the WILKESBARRE and the pair headed east. There was five feet of water in the SMITH's hold and her crew made busy at the hand pumps, squirting as much as possible over the side.

When the WILKESBARRE and her crippled consort arrived in Buffalo, Captain Trudo offered what he claimed to be the WILKESBARRE's compensation for the short tow, 100 dollars. The WILKESBARRE's master, however, claimed that the deal was for 700 dollars. It had been a scant distance from where the schooner was adrift to the Buffalo dock, and in 1907 terms this was a whopping sum of money. Captain Trudo refused to pay, and an extremely heated scene ensued. In the end the owners of the WILKESBARRE libelled the ANGUS SMITH for 5000 dollars. The schooner was arrested at her dock, a rather pointless measure, considering that with several feet of water still in her hold and a gaping hole in her deck, the ANGUS SMITH was not going any place.

It took nearly two weeks for Captain Trudo to make temporary repairs and bond his boat out of arrest. By the time the ANGUS SMITH again set out for Bay City, the WILKESBARRE had long since resumed her normal duties around the lakes. This time Captain Trudo was having no part of tows for hire and raised the boat's sails. For the next week, the schooner limped toward Mr. Clute's dock on the Saginaw River. On Thursday the 22nd of November, she picked up a tug at the river's mouth and made her way to discharge her cargo.

The ANGUS SMITH was taken to the Bay City shipyard of James Davidson for thorough repairs. The boat was a sight when she was pushed into the slip—with her cabin twisted from the hull, anchors missing, planking broken, a fallen mast on her deck and a yawning hole where it had once been. The SMITH represented a fair amount of winter work for Mr. Davidson's ship yard employees. For Captain Trudo's strongbox the whole fiasco had been a major strain. With the expense of the repairs, the bond, the pending suit and the tow of the CHARLES A. EDDY, Captain Trudo found himself considerably less liquid. The SMITH would spend the winter at Bay City and the following spring try for a more profitable season. Captain Trudo no doubt would keep his floating business under its own sails long enough to pay for the previous autumn's losses. When making future transactions for towing, he would always keep in mind that a deal is not always a deal.

The Ketcham Blockade

*I*n the final years of the 1890s the flow of traffic between Lakes Huron and Superior had become smooth through the Soo. With giant new locks now open, the days of vessels having to tie up and wait in line to lock up and down were at last gone. The opening of the original Poe lock in 1896 and the Canadian lock the year before had reduced the normal crowds of waiting vessels to, at worst a steady trickle. And transformation of the Soo occurred, as it turned from a place to sit and wait, to a place to briefly pass through. In 1894 the annual flow of iron ore through the Soo was 7,748,932 tons, but within four years the tonnage had nearly doubled to a whopping 14,024,673 tons. If the growth rate continued, the tonnage figures were projected to top the 40 million ton mark by 1910. Those who governed the ship canal could not have felt more satisfied. Just one bottleneck remained and that was the Saint Marys River itself. The only passage for lake boats past Neebish Island was the narrow confines of the Munuscong Channel to the east, and both upbound and downbound boats had to squeeze through its half-mile wide gap at Johnson Point.

The fifth of September, 1899 was a typical autumn day at the Soo. Vessels were passing upbound and downbound with the beat of their routine rhythms. In the traffic steamed the Bessemer Steamship Company's 475 foot steel monster DOUGLASS HOUGHTON, downbound with a belly full of ore. Firmly attached to the three-month-old steamer's stern, by nearly two boat lengths of towing hawser, was her 450 foot consort, the steel barge JOHN FRITZ with an identical ore cargo. Suddenly, when just above Johnson Point, the HOUGHTON's steering apparatus failed and her wheel spun without response. Her master reacted quickly by checking the boat's speed to a crawl and preparing to drop her hooks. Carried by the law of inertia and the current of the Saint Mary's River, on came the ore filled FRITZ and slammed into the HOUGHTON's stern. In short order, the HOUGHTON was resting on the bottom and traffic on the river came to a halt.

From that Tuesday until the following Sunday, the "Houghton Blockade" went on. More than 100 lakeboats were trapped above and below the channel until the HOUGHTON was raised. The whole ordeal shook the ship canal authorities to their roots, and everyone knew that something had to be done. Lakeboats were not only growing larger, but more numerous with each passing season, and another blockade might be of greater duration, and could send ripples through the industrial northeast. In the following years came a proposal for a second channel to the west of Neebish Island to allow vessel passage, should a mishap occur in the east channel. Completed in 1908, the "Rock Cut" opened the West Neebish Channel to navigation. It was determined that the old "Sailors Encampment" channel to the east would be used by upbounders and the new West Neebish Channel by downbounders. Surely the problems of another blockade were now eliminated.

When it comes to conditions of weather and how it is logged by vesselmen, one particular term has always been avoided with great intent, that is the reference to "fog". Mariners have always seemed to exchange the word "fog" for the preferred term "haze". The reasoning here is that boats running in fog would have to be checked to slow, or stopped completely, while a vessel running in haze would have no such constraints. Additionally, should there be any type of accident, the word fog written into a logbook would raise countless questions. So interchangeable have become the terms, that the two could be considered to have the same meaning. This has carried forward into modern times, a case in point being a September 18, 1988 radio conversation between the Algoma Central Railway's big self-unloader AGAWA

CANYON, and the dredge NORTHERLY ISLAND. The CANYON was inbound up the Saginaw River and the NORTHERLY ISLAND outbound for the pump-out station just beyond the river's mouth. A thick layer of low fog was hanging over the entire area as the 646 foot AGAWA CANYON crept carefully into the river, using her radar and every bit of caution appropriate to the situation, and then some. The same care was conducted by the dredge. The conversation between the two masters never once used the word "fog". Initially the dredge reported the conditions in the river as "a little haze...at least a mile visibility..." Later, the Zilwaukee Bridge tender reported to the AGAWA CANYON that it was "...pretty soupy up here, we can't hardly even see the crossbars with the stop lights on..." The CANYON herself reported the visibility as 100 feet to the dredge, who responded that it was zero on the bay. Through the skill of her master and the quality of her equipment the CANYON made her dock as a matter of routine that morning, but the term "fog" was never uttered, the conditions described only as "haze". On Friday evening the 20th day of May, 1910 a fair bit of "haze" had settled in about the Saint Marys River as the steamer JOHN B. KETCHAM II headed downbound. She was just one of the 20,899 passages through the Soo that year.

Pulpwood was the cargo that the KETCHAM was bringing down from the upper lakes, her hold stuffed full and an additional 350 cords stacked on her deck. Constructed in 1892, the 909 ton wooden steamer measured 193 feet long and was the property of H. M. Loud & Co. of Au Sable, Michigan. This "hazy" afternoon she was following closely behind another H. M. Loud boat, the 226 foot wooden steamer KONGO. The two boats were simply picking their way through the foggy day, with none of the technology that the AGAWA CANYON would enjoy 78 seasons into the future.

As the pair of wooden steamers made their way below Nine Mile Point and completed the turn into the West Neebish Channel, the KONGO strayed from the channel and stuck her

The John B. Ketcham II would become the boat that would slow the traffic through the Soo locks to a crawl and frustrate superintendent L.C. Sabin to no end.

bow firmly in the mud. With a swerve that only a boat of her size could muster, the KETCHAM avoided slamming into the stuck steamer. Stopping a few boat-lengths below the KONGO, the KETCHAM backed cautiously to aid her fleetmate, and perhaps save the company the expense of a tug. A line was rigged between the stern of the KETCHAM and that of the stricken KONGO. Surges of thick black coal smoke mixed with the day's fog as the KETCHAM hauled on the KONGO. Churning muddy water, the screws of both boats dug for freedom. Creaking and twisting, the towing hawser stretched bar tight, but the KONGO refused to budge. Shifting from upstream to downstream, the KETCHAM hauled back and forth on the boat's heels, but without result. The KONGO was stuck fast and a boat with more maneuverability would be required to free her.

From the Soo the tug GENERAL was summoned and promptly the KONGO was pulled from the river's muddy bottom. Once more the KONGO proceeded toward the Rock Cut, followed by the KETCHAM which had been standing by upstream. The plan was for the two vessels to proceed as far as the cut, where the KONGO would tie up and be inspected. Separating from her runningmate, the KETCHAM would proceed alone. As the pair began to move down, two other lakeboats joined the foggy parade. Catching up came the wooden oreboat LOUISIANA and the steel steamer ALVA.

Dropping off to the side, the KONGO prepared to tie up above the cut, while the KETCHAM moved to enter the channel. Just before eight o'clock in the evening, the KETCHAM's starboard bow slammed solidly into the crib at the dam near the mouth of the upper Rock Cut. For an instant she jolted to a stop, when the current grabbed her stern and began to swing her sideways across the channel. The closely-following LOUISIANA had little choice other than plowing ahead into the narrow Rock Cut, for if she reversed, the ALVA would ram her from behind. Aboard the ALVA, the whole mess was still obscured by the fog.

In minutes the current was dragging the KETCHAM nearly 180 degrees around. Anticipating this, the LOUISIANA's master, Captain Fred McDonald, made a desperate but effective move. Throwing the boat's chadburn to "ahead full," he grabbed the wheel himself and swung the 275 foot steamer to port. Squeezing as far to the east as he dared, it was his intent to pass the tumbling KETCHAM in the brief moments when her hull was parallel in the channel. The LOUISIANA's wooden hull struck hard against the cut as she squeaked by the KETCHAM and the ALVA followed, doing the same. Like a closing gate, the KETCHAM's hull continued around, the stern crunching into the boulders 50 feet from the west shore. Her punctured bow swung to within 40 feet of the east bank and promptly sank. The new Rock Cut and the West Neebish Channel were blockaded by the KETCHAM.

At Sault Saint Marie ship canal Superintendent L. C. Sabin was peacefully snoozing Friday night into Saturday morning. A normal half day of work Saturday would lead him into a relaxing spring weekend. Now that winter's ice was finally clear of the river and locks, he was looking forward to a smooth summer of maritime commerce under his command. Perhaps his sleep was even filled with dreamy images of lakeboats flowing unrestricted through the three locks and surrounding waterways.

A little past four a. m. Superintendent Sabin's bliss, as well as his weekend, was shattered by a persistent pounding at his front door. An hour later he was boarding the government tug, and by five o'clock the tug with Mr. Sabin was on its way to the wreck site. Steaming ahead was the tug GENERAL which had brought the news of the blockade up from the cut. Onboard her was Captain Root of the Great Lakes Towing & Wrecking Company and Superintendent C. G. Lampman of the Pittsburgh Steamship Company on their way to a tangle that they all believed could be quickly undone.

Reaching the cut after first light, the two tugs came upon a monumental mess. A snarl of downbound vessels had stopped and dropped their hooks above the cut. The KONGO sat just outside the channel somewhat caught in the middle. Licking their wounds below the cut rested the LOUISIANA and ALVA. Finally, stretched smack across the channel was the KETCHAM. Her bow and stern were within a stone toss of each bank, and her fo'c'sle deck and after cabin roof were only three feet above the water. Worst of all, her spar deck was a good eight feet under water and all that was visible was part of the 350 cords of wood stacked upon it. Surveying the impasse, Superintendent Sabin removed his hat and slowly ran his hand over the top of his head. His weekend was definitely shot.

Completing their survey of the wreck, Captain Root and Superintendent Sabin returned to the locks administration building at noon. Along the walk from the lower pier, they devised a plan of attack. First the KETCHAM's deckload would be removed and tugs would pull her bow around so that vessels could pass, and divers would patch her bow so that she could be pumped out and floated to drydock. At two o'clock Saturday afternoon the tugs GENERAL and SCHENCK headed down from the Government dock with a task force of 17 men to unload the KETCHAM. Arms folded and chin high, Foreman J. B. Audette stood at the bow of the GENERAL. He was determined to make short work of clearing the wreck's deck cargo, assuring Mr. Sabin that the work gang would be back to the Soo by dinner time.

Approaching the cut, the plan of attack was quickly put into action. Foreman Audette first directed that a string of boom sticks be set downstream across the lower end of the cut to catch the pulpwood that would be jettisoned from the KETCHAM. Next the GENERAL and SCHENCK bumped up to the submerged wreck and the platoon of laborers climbed atop the stack of pulpwood. Under Foreman Audette's command they assaulted the stack and one after another ragged poles of pulpwood splashed into the swift Saint Marys River.

A deep trench had been dug through the center of the pile and the river's current began to shift the load, so the team withdrew and let the river do the work. Steadily the pulpwood pivoted, swayed and collapsed over the side. Just as the laborers were congratulating one another on a job well done, they realized that the nearly 300 cords of remaining pulpwood were charging downstream toward the containment booms in two massive clumps. The group's elation faded as the tangled mass plowed through the string of boom sticks with a snap and scattered downstream. The logs were now free to foul sidewheels, screws, rudders and to puncture the wooden hulls of unsuspecting lakeboats. Foreman Audette had finished before dinner, but it was a mixed victory. Next the tugs positioned themselves to pull the boat around. With the GENERAL and SCHENCK hauling on the KETCHAM's bow, the struggle began.

Meanwhile, back up at the Soo, Superintendent Sabin was keeping atop the situation. Vessels were already stacking up at the locks and more were crowding above the cut. Mr. Sabin sent a wire to Port Huron requesting that the big wrecking tug FAVORITE be dispatched to the scene. He directed that upbound boats would use the Encampment channel at night and downbounders during the daylight hours. No vessel was to pass the narrow turn at Johnson Point without escort of the tug BOYNTON. The tug was assigned the task of helping in any other way required by the blockade.

The BOYNTON was called away from her escort duties late Saturday when the GENERAL and SCHENCK managed to move the KETCHAM some four feet. Captain Root believed that a third tug hauling on the boat's stern might bring her around. Upon her arrival, the BOYNTON tied to the crippled steamer's heels, and with plumes of thick black smoke, the tug-of-war started once more. Despite the tremendous power being applied to the KETCHAM, she refused to budge. And with her engine at full ahead, the BOYNTON's line to the KETCHAM suddenly snapped. The tug tumbled drunkenly down the cut and slammed several times into the rocks along the bank. By the time she had been brought back under control, her keel had been split and her sternpost, rudder and shoe bent. Dejectedly, the wounded BOYNTON limped to the Soo and a friendly drydock. It was quickly becoming clear that the KETCHAM blockade would not easily be cleared.

Joining the crowd of boats anchored in Hay Lake above the Rock Cut, and waiting for the mess to be sorted out, came the Wolvin Line's H. P. BOPE. Her Master had been told of the blockade while locking down, and of the restriction to downbounders imposed by Superintendent Sabin. Night had just fallen and that meant that the Encampment channel was now supposed to be open to only upbound vessels. As the BOPE's master looked over the gaggle of more than two dozen vessels already backed up above the cut, he knew that his boat would have to wait not only until daylight, but perhaps through the following day for his turn to pass down. This situation did not sit well with the BOPE's captain, not well at all. He was not about to allow

Superintendent Sabin to delay his boat for an entire day, not by a damn sight. With a muttered, gruff scoff he began to back the BOPE up the river to just above Sand Island. Like an impatient yuppie in a traffic jam he headed the 552 foot steamer the wrong way down the Middle Neebish and Munuscong Channels.

In the hour that followed, the BOPE had passed a number of confused upbounders. Her master was favoring the west side of the channel in order to keep opposing boats well to port. Feeling clever for having gotten the jump on the crowd in Hay Lake, the H. P. BOPE's captain unfortunately got what he deserved just before nine o'clock Saturday night. Off Mirre Point, above the "Dark Hole," the BOPE's bow found a shoal and ran hard aground. Her stern swinging with the current, the steamer came to rest across the channel. Once again, a frantic knocking at his door disturbed Superintendent Sabin, who had been attempting to regain the sleep he had lost the previous night. This time the messenger meekly informed the Superintendent that his entire seaway was cut off.

By one o'clock Sunday morning the tug GENERAL had succeeded in pulling the BOPE around clear of the channel, but it took another three hours to get her floating again. Under the escort of the tug the steamer headed back to the Soo where she would be inspected and her captain would meet with a tired, irritable Superintendent Sabin to answer some well-deserved questions. Sunday morning saw the Superintendent sending to engage the services of Captain James Reid, the wizard of Great Lakes salvage. Captain Reid, who had been working on the sunken HENRY STEINBRENNER in the lower Saint Marys River, came up to the Soo and met with the Superintendent Sunday afternoon. The deal was promptly closed and Captain Reid left the Soo late that same day and went directly to the KETCHAM. More than 100 lakeboats were now crowded above the Rock Cut. Quick evaluation of the wreck led Captain Reid to send back to Port Huron for a pair of salvage pontoons to lift the KETCHAM's bow. He then wasted no time in halting work on the KETCHAM.

He had been working on the STEINBRENNER for a long time and almost had her raised. Nothing more could be done in the cut until the pontoons arrived from Port Huron.

At 9:40 Monday morning the tug WINSLOW was logged as passing upbound at Port Huron, with Captain Reid's requested pontoons in tow. Heavy fog on Lake Huron, as well as the fact that the floats could only be towed slowly, would hamper the tug's trip. On Thursday the STEINBRENNER was surfaced and taken to De Tour. The following morning the tug WINSLOW was recorded passing that same point at five o'clock with the pontoons in tow. Superintendent Sabin got the word from Captain Reid that as soon as the pontoons reached the cut, they would be put to use raising the KETCHAM. Mr. Sabin was confident the famous Captain Reid would make short work of the wreck, and the Superintendent could finally have that restful weekend he had been robbed of on that "hazy" May evening seven days before. Leaning back in his big office chair, he could feel the burden beginning to lift from his shoulders.

May turned into June, the two pontoons had turned into four and Superintendent Sabin's aggravation turned into daily routine. The steamer JOHN B. KETCHAM II remained firmly stuck across the Rock Cut. The passage of vessels up and down the Encampment channel had become so easy that boats were experiencing less than 15 minutes delay in most cases. Luckily, Captain Reid was not a man who would let the pressures of a busy seaway interfere with working a wreck. He knew that the greater the degree of patience applied to a sunken vessel, the better the odds that it would float once more. Such was the philosophy of a good "wrecker."

Finally on Friday the 10th of June, 1910 the KETCHAM stirred from her resting place. With her bow buoyed up by four pontoons and two tugs snorting on her prow, the steamer was swung clear of the boulders. With a tug on each end she was pulled down below the cut. At once the word went up to Superintendent Sabin, who by now was just too tired to feel relieved. A steady flow of downbound oreboats began to move through Rock Cut. One after another, the lakers pushed silently past the sorrowful hulk of the JOHN B. KETCHAM II, sitting in a list on the west riverbank, surrounded by tugs, and with pontoons still attached to her nose. On each freighter, sailors would stand at the rail to get a look at the wreck as they passed. Doubtless, the comment could be heard—"all that on account of a little haze."

Tawas Point
and Vessels Gone By

*A*ll five of the Great Lakes, when viewed from anywhere, are beautiful things to ponder, and each seems to have its own best vantage points. When visiting Lake Huron, on the Michigan side, an excellent place to stop is the Tawas State Park. A daily pass gets the visitor in to the sandy park beach. Walking along the beach, it is easy to see Big Charity Island some 16 miles south, as well as Little Charity Island another half mile south. Standing there in the sand and gazing out over the blue lake, you can envision vessels gone by, storm winds blowing, boats run ashore and sailors in peril. When doing so, use your most vivid imagination and know that your thoughts are not far off.

On the tenth day of April 1890, the wooden package freighter CHENANGO began her first trip of the season. Bound from Detroit to Buffalo with a hold full of wheat, the 182 foot steamer cleared what remained of the Detroit River's ice and plowed around on an east-bound course. Late on the day of the 11th, the CHENANGO was hauling just off Erie, Pennsylvania, when fire was discovered in the timbers adjacent to her boilers. In less than an hour, the boat's after accommodations were ablaze. The flames and smoke drew the attention of the passing boat EBER WARD, which pulled near and attempted to help fight the fire. The TECUMSECH arrived on the scene and joined the effort. Things quickly began to look hopeless, and it was decided to tow the burning lakeboat into the port of Erie and scuttle her in shallow water. As the WARD and TECUMSECH neared Erie, the fire was winning the race, and seemed about to consume the CHENANGO completely. She was scuttled just short of port.

The CHENANGO's crew were taken to Toledo by the WARD, and the burned-out hulk of the steamer was left to the underwriters. Three months later, shipping wizard James Davidson raised the hulk, and on the first of July towed her to a dock on the north side of the Buffalo River. He removed what remained of her scorched wheat cargo and took what was left of the steamer to his Bay City, Michigan shipyard. The boat was a frightful sight and many vesselmen expressed the opinion that she was simply not worth the effort and would never sail again. Over the winter the CHENANGO's remains were rebuilt into the familiar form of a lumber hooker, and her new measurements were 175 feet in overall length, 34 feet in beam and 13 feet in depth. She sported a new profile, with a box-like pilothouse atop her fo'c'sle, a clear spar deck for piling on cargo, and engine accommodations aft. The summer following her disastrous fire, she sailed from Bay City with her new look—and a new name, LIZZIE MADDEN.

Some 17 seasons after the LIZZIE MADDEN's brush with destruction she was still earning her way along the Great Lakes. Tuesday, November 19, 1907 found the MADDEN rounding Michigan's thumb from Lake Huron, inbound to Bay City with 800 tons of Tonawanda hard coal in her belly. In command on this low, dull autumn day was Captain Ralph Pringle. It was his goal, not only to deliver the MADDEN's cargo to the Boutell Brothers dock, but to cross Saginaw Bay ahead of the worsening weather. A fairly nasty batch of fall weather was beginning to show its teeth, and Captain Pringle wanted no part of it, if at all possible. The MADDEN was producing lots of good black smoke, as she pushed her way to the mouth of the Saginaw River.

This was the little steamer's first arrival into Bay City in two years—an unusual fact considering that her owners, the T. F. Madden estate, and operators, M. J. Lynn were both of Bay City. A decline in "king lumber" along the Saginaw river had forced the boat into the Georgian Bay, Tonawanda route. Now the steamer had grabbed a convenient cargo to allow her to visit

Seen here at the Soo locks in better days, the LIZZIE MADDEN would find her end below Tawas Point on a stormy November night.

home port, as if anyone would notice in the crowded river. To most, the LIZZIE MADDEN was simply another hooting whistle, and another smoking stack on the waterway. Shortly after tying up at the Boutell dock, the laborious bucket-and-tackle task of unloading began. More quickly unloaded were watchman Willfred Lacomb, wheelsman Charles Crashaw and seaman Merton Gilroy, all of whom were Bay City residents. This stop gave them a rare opportunity to visit home, and considering that it would take nearly two days to unload, they would even get the chance to get reacquainted with their families.

As the MADDEN stood moored firmly to the unloading dock, the fall winds began to grow to gale force. By Wednesday afternoon Saginaw Bay had been churned into a fitful tantrum. The wind was howling from the southeast at more than 30 miles per hour and seas of nearly 12 feet were marching up the bay.

Downbound into the teeth of the storm came the schooner-barge G. K. JACKSON faithfully following her towing steamer.

Stacked high atop the barge's deck was a cargo of rough-cut lumber consigned to a Saginaw dock. After the fall of darkness Wednesday night, the JACKSON's towline parted and the boat fell adrift. Taking the problem in hand, sailor Theron Kent climbed atop the fo'c'sle to attempt to reconnect the line. The seas swept him over the side and in a heartbeat the icy lake swallowed him forever. And the waves began to take advantage of the boat's cargo, plundering it layer by layer, as the helpless barge was driven before the storm. In the darkness, the waves mixed with the lumber caved in the fo'c'sle and showered the crew with cascades of wood, jumbled with icewater. By the time the deckload was picked to the rails, the schooner's wooden hull came crashing ashore on Tawas Park beach. Through the numbing November night the JACKSON's crew fought to survive—in the exact place where modern vacationers stroll and collect rocks.

Lake Michigan was driven into a rage, too, and along its full length the lakeboats ran for cover. By Thursday morning the new breakwater at Muskegon was suffering greatly. Construction of the breakwater had been contracted to Nelson J. Gaylord of Ludington whose employees had done an exceptional job. Now they could do little but stand back and watch the lake pick it apart, when without explanation, 40 year old carpenter Gustave Paul started out onto the break wall. Just what he thought he could do out there for his employer, Mr. Gaylord, will forever be unknown. The carpenter struggled toward the end of the wall and vanished into the maelstrom.

With the storm winds shifting from the southeast to southwest on Thursday morning, the lee of the land allowed the Tawas lifesavers enough protection to get to the stranded G. K. JACKSON. It was a bitter cold, numbing operation, but the schooner-barge's crew were removed to the warmth of the lifesaving station. As a group they recovered swiftly and were transported to Bay City by the JACKSON's steamer.

Friday the 22nd of November saw the winds decrease to a modest blow on Saginaw Bay. Shortly before 4 o'clock in the afternoon the LIZZIE MADDEN cast off, light, for Little Current, Ontario. A cargo of fresh-cut Canadian lumber waited there for a routine Tonawanda delivery. As the MADDEN hissed, bow-high, onto the bay her prow found only an ugly chop left by the storm. Captain Pringle pointed his boat on the upbound course for Georgian Bay and prepared for a routine trip.

In the wake of the MADDEN's departure from the Boutell dock, the lumber hooker LANGELL BOYS took her place. The 160 foot steamer was to take on coal bunkers from the pile that the MADDEN had just left behind. Coaling of the boat was completed in the better part of four hours, and the LANGELL BOYS, like the MADDEN, started out of the river and up Saginaw Bay. The time the LANGELL BOYS had taken at the coal dock put her a bit more than 15 miles behind the LIZZIE MADDEN. By the time the LANGELL BOYS tasted the first of Saginaw Bay's chop, the MADDEN was but a smudge over the horizon.

From the MADDEN's pilothouse, Captain Pringle was spotting on the Charity Island light through the new-fallen darkness. As the good captain was reassuring himself of his position, the pilothouse door came open and the cold winds from the bay spilled in. Standing spread-eagle was watchman Smith, his face flush-red. "Captain,...there's smoke all below!" Captain Pringle slammed the engine telegraph to "stop" and blew a series of short blasts on the MADDEN's whistle to wake all hands. As the captain, wheelsman and watchman bounded down the ladder, the smell of smoke grew stronger. Reaching the spar deck, they found the companionway doors open and a fog of smoke filling the fo'c'sle. Fighting their way forward, the crewmen found the lantern room a blazing purgatory, with flames beginning to run to the ceiling. The heat and smoke forced everyone out on deck, coughing and with eyes tearing. Hoses were promptly rigged to the boat's pumps and fighting of the fire began in an orderly fashion. As if using a squirt gun on a campfire, the hoses and pumps had no effect on the spreading inferno. Soon the entire bow was threatened, flames licking between the seams of the

MADDEN's planking, and through the forward windows. The
men could feel the fire spreading through the empty cargo hold
beneath their feet. Directing their meager hose downward, they
were being forced aft.

From the pilothouse of the LANGELL BOYS a flickering
orange glow like a small sunrise could be seen on the horizon.
The captain knew in the blink of an eye that a vessel was ablaze
just over the horizon, and the odds were good that the burning
boat was the LIZZIE MADDEN. The order was rung for full
steam, and the LANGELL BOYS churned a froth. As the glow
grew more intense, the pilothouse called down for more steam,
and the pressure built to the point where the safety valve
opened. To the rescue the LANGELL BOYS pressed, safety valve
poppin' all the way.

Onboard the burning LIZZIE MADDEN, the situation had
become impossible. Attention now had to be shifted from fighting
the fire to launching the boats. The flames had consumed the
firehose and were on the verge of consuming the after quarters,
atop which the lifeboats were still secured. Captain Pringle must
either launch 'em or lose 'em, so both boats went over the side.
No sooner had the boats hit the water than the crew was forced
to follow, with flames at their heels. Captain Pringle found to his
dismay that his boat was without a compass, requiring him to
return to the after cabin roof and attempt to grab the emergency
compass. Fighting his way through the fire and smoke, he got
the device and was forced to walk the rail and shimmy down the
falls, like a circus road-hand, to get back to the lifeboat. Both
boats rowed off into the rough bay in two different directions.
Once away from the glow of the burning MADDEN they were
blended into darkness. Captain Pringle's boat pulled for Point
Lookout, while the mate's boat pulled for the Charity Island light
about four miles off.

A short time after the lifeboats had moved off into the darkness, the LANGELL BOYS pulled onto the scene. To insure that
none of the airborne embers from the now fully-engulfed MAD-

DEN would catch their boat, the rescue steamer stood well off. At first the scene was quite puzzling—only a drifting, burning derelict, with no signs of life what-so-ever. The LANGELL BOYS started in a long, wide, dead-slow circle looking for survivors and repeatedly hooting the whistle, when before long her probing searchlight fell upon Captain Pringle's boat. The occupants were taken aboard and the yawl hoisted to the deck one hour after abandoning the MADDEN. Less than an hour later the second boat showed up, having heard the LANGELL BOYS whistle and turned back for the MADDEN's glow. With all of the castaways safe aboard, the LANGELL BOYS steamed for East Tawas. As they pulled away, all aboard took one last look at the once proud LIZZIE MADDEN, now burned nearly to the water line and drifting westward toward Little Charity Island about four miles off. At one o'clock Saturday morning November 23, 1907 the LANGELL BOYS pulled up to the dilapidated Tawas dock to discharge the MADDEN's crew. The same day Mr. Lynn, the MADDEN's manager, met the crew at the Bay City train station and treated the group to dinner as well as a round of affidavit-signing to close out the career of the LIZZIE MADDEN.

Nearly 24 years after the LIZZIE MADDEN's career had come to an end, Captain Bert Payee guided the lumber hooker LANGELL BOYS onto the range lights that would lead him to the mouth of the Saginaw River, and uttered a resigned sigh. It was a sultry afternoon, the second week of June, 1931, and the Saginaw River was a vastly different place for Captain Payee and his tiny oak steamer than in years before. Entering the once bustling river revealed the signs of the deepening economic depression, a sharp contrast to the river's salad days of the lumber boom.

Just three years from her launch in 1890 at Simon Langell's St. Clair, Michigan shipyard, the LANGELL BOYS was sold to Bay City interests going to work for the Bradley fleet. In her heyday the LANGELL BOYS would often log as many as three passages a week in and out of the Saginaw River. With great efficiency the little steamer worked the Canadian lumber camps that lined Georgian Bay. Filling her hold and stacked deckhouse high on her deck, the lumber hooker could carry more than half a million board feet of product back from the camps. If need be, the LANGELL BOYS could haul 500 tons of coal or any other bulk cargo back up to the wilderness shore. In addition, her powerful engine allowed for the towing of consort barges, enhancing her efficiency. Before the turn of the century she was regularly seen pulling the schooner-barges J. B. COMSTOCK and ABRAM SMITH. In October of 1906, however, the three were caught in a Lake Huron gale that wrecked the two barges but left the LANGELL BOYS to sail another day.

Throughout her career the LANGELL BOYS changed owners multiple times, yet her home port seemed to be always on the Saginaw River and she normally hauled her cargos across Lake Huron. Captain Payee came upon her decks in 1915 and found himself a home. Five years later, a dock-side fire nearly destroyed their relationship when it consumed the LANGELL BOYS to her spar deck. She was towed from Saginaw to Marine City, Michigan and rebuilt at the McClouth yard. The 30 year old steamer was given roomier deck houses and her looks were altered slightly during the rebuild. In tonnage the reflected difference was from 387 tons up to 467 tons. A season later, she had returned to the Saginaw River and her lumber-moving duties.

By 1931 the lumbering industry, as well as the era of the wooden lakeboat, had come to a grinding dissolve. As the LANGELL BOYS hissed slowly through Bay City, she passed the corpses left behind by the worsening economic times. Along nearly the entire length of the Saginaw River rested the hulks of once productive lakeboats. Some were in indefinite lay-up, waiting for an economic turn around that, unknown to anyone, was nearly a decade in the future. Other boats were abandoned where they had last tied up, their parent companies having evaporated with the rest of the planet's economy. Many of the

Seen here in winter lay-up and after her 1920 rebuild, the LAN-GELL BOYS was such a common sight along the Saginaw River that most people didn't notice her passing. That was also true in 1931 when she passed for the last time.

wooden boats would, in years to come, turn into a source of shelter for persons with shattered lives, or firewood for shivering families who could not afford food, let alone coal for heat. The once busy fleet on a once busy waterway now sat sorry, soon to rust and rot. There was no escape. This was the state of the world.

Gazing from the pilothouse of the LANGELL BOYS Captain Payee was too numbed by the current way of the world to be further disheartened by the bleakness that surrounded him. In fact the LANGELL BOYS, which in good times made three trips a week, was returning from only her third trip of the two and a half month old season. With career mariners out of work, the good captain was simply relieved that his was not one of the wooden lakers listing in the mud along the riverbank. Two companies, the Mershon Eddy Parker interests as well as the Carrollton Steamship Company, had applied a fresh coat of red paint to the LANGELL BOYS, and were running her. What meager lumber business they could scrounge would fill her hold.

The steamer's crew of 12 were glad to get what work she could provide. They knew all too well that each of the derelict boats they saw everywhere along the lakes once had a crew. Hard times meant a lot of sailors on the beach and luck was with the seaman who was still gainfully employed. Even with her current service, the future did not look good for the little wooden lakeboat. For the most part every one had the feeling that they were working on a trip-by-trip basis. As the LANGELL BOYS approached the Mershon dock, Captain Payee knew that her last trip might not be far off.

Tying up to the Mershon Eddy dock the LANGELL BOYS brought welcome work to the gang waiting to unload her. Waiting at the dock was Mr. Arthur H. Hempstead with an overnight bag poised at his feet. Other than being a good friend of Captain Payee, Mr. Hempstead was president of the Mershon Eddy Parker Lumber Company. Boarding the LANGELL BOYS, Mr. Hempstead was greeted by Captain Payee with a brisk handshake, and the two made their way to the captain's office for a strategy session. Making the trip to Blind River, Ontario, Mr. Hempstead would be performing some on-site wheeling and dealing, in an attempt to secure the continued flow of timber across his company docks.

By noon on Saturday June 13th, 1931 the cargo of the LANGELL BOYS had been neatly stacked upon the Mershon dock and her crew had set to work securing her six foot by 11 foot hatches. The boat's lines had already been cast off and her bow pointed toward the middle of the murky Saginaw River. By the time all three of the boat's hatches had been closed, the steamer was hissing peaceful up the bending portion of the river between Zilwaukee and Bay City. Surrounded by deep green trees and pastures, the quiet was interrupted solely by the occasional buzz of an insect spiraling past. From the pilothouse of the LANGELL BOYS it was easy for Captain Payee to lose the troubles of the times, at least for the moment, in this glorious summer afternoon.

At half past four the little red steamer passed from the confines of the Saginaw River and onto the widening expanse of Saginaw Bay. By the time dinner was finished both Mr. Hempstead and Captain Payee were standing at the boat's worn wooden rail gazing across the bay. In the hazy distance the Michigan shore slipped past along with the captain's home town of Standish. Soon the spike of Point au Gres should appear off the port quarter, and the LANGELL BOYS would easily pass between Point Lookout and Big and Little Charity Islands. From shore, cabin dwellers gave little notice to the tiny steamer silhouetted against the dusk, trailing black smoke. To them she was just another lakeboat, one of the shrinking fleet of working lakers.

When darkness began to settle upon the LANGELL BOYS the flashing of the lighthouse on Tawas Point was clearly visible from the steamer's pilothouse. The steamer's course would hug the Michigan shore, rounding until just off Thunder Bay. There the LANGELL BOYS would turn nearly due north and, between four and five o'clock Sunday morning, pass close enough to North Point to almostly feel the rocks. From there it would be a straight haul to Mississagi Strait, with the boat passing up in the noon hour. All of this added up to the LANGELL BOYS being due at Blind River about 24 hours after clearing Bay City. But as the evening grew late, the tidy schedule of the little red lakeboat was about to be radically changed.

Just after nine o'clock a crewman discovered a smoky haze hovering about the steamer's spar deck. Hastily, hands were mustered to investigate the source of the strange smoke. The roof of the aft deck house was checked first, as it was there that wooden steamers were most prone to catch fire. Sparks from a boat's stack would lodge between it and the wooden cabin, glowing until their time for bursting into flames. The roof was clear and the quest for the smoldering extended to the cabins, concentrating around the engine room and fire hold. Still nothing conclusive was found, while on deck the smoke was growing ominously thick.

At length the boat's hatches were opened to allow inspection of her hold. A wind, nearing gale force, blasted down through the opening, and at the boat's coal bunker, purgatory burst forth. The fire had started at the base of the fuel bunker and had been waiting for the draft provided by the open hatches to come alive. The 41 year old timbers of the boat's lower hull were quite tender, and readily ignited. By the time the searching crewmen scrambled from the hold, the LANGELL BOYS appeared to be a lost cause.

From the Au Sable shoreline, residents began to notice a growing fire out on the lake. Closer squinting revealed the lights of a vessel, mounted upon the floating bonfire. As the distant fire began to grow in intensity, so did the concern of the crowd growing on the beach. By 10 o'clock the telephone at the Tawas Coast Guard Station began to ring continuously. Stepping outside, the Coast Guardsmen could see the glow out on the lake to the north. In a hustle they got underway with their boat and headed for the distant fire. For those onboard the rescue boat, the trip around Tawas Point was a nerve-twisting experience, for it seemed to take hours to get to the open lake. Rounding the point they sighted on the flaring horizon. At times they swore that they smelled the smoke, but considering that the LANGELL BOYS was still a dozen miles off, that was not likely.

An hour an a half after the Tawas coast guard station's phone first began to ring, the rescue boat reached the flaming LANGELL BOYS. They discovered the boat's hulk totally involved in flame and not a soul to be rescued. Orbiting the wreck, they could make out that her life boat davits had been cranked out and the boats were gone. Figuring that the crew had abandoned the steamer and were rowing for shore, the coast guardsmen started a zigzag search toward Au Sable Point. Minutes into their search, they picked up the wayward crew and brought them back to Tawas. The LANGELL BOYS, or at least what remained of her, was left to burn on Lake Huron. Captain Payee and his crew made their way home to join the growing ranks of the unemployed. Mr. Hempstead simply returned to Saginaw to try to calculate the next move for the Mershon Eddy Parker Company.

Today, little remains of the events off the Tawas shore. The G. K. JACKSON was pulled free of Tawas Point, and returned to service. What remained of the MADDEN came to rest off Little Charity Island, and in later years her machinery was salvaged. Today, her bones have been scoured clean by modern-day scuba divers. The charred remains of the LANGELL BOYS came to rest just north of the point off the Au Sable shore. All of the participants in the MADDEN's drama have long since passed. But, after reading this story, if you walk out on Tawas Point, look out onto the lake and daydream a bit. You just may find some images of fires...storms...waves...lifesavers...and vessels gone by.

Reference Sources

A STYLISH PATCH FOR THE GREAT LAKES CRAZY QUILT
REF; Bay City Tribune 10/15/1902
"Namesakes 1900-1909"; Greenwood
"Namesakes II"; Greenwood
"Lake Superior, The American Lakes Series," Nute
"Pigboat...The Story Of The Whalebacks," Lydecker
"Freshwater Whales," Wright

THE GHOST SHIP OF YANKEE REEF
REF; Bay City Tribune 11/27,28,29,30/1891, 12/1/1891
Bay City Times 7/1/1890
"Namesakes 1900-1909,1910-1919,1920-1929"
Greenwood
"Shipwrecks Of Lake Huron," Parker
"Great Lakes Ships We Remember,I" Van der Linden
"Lake Huron, The American Lakes Series," Landon
Phone conversation with Martha Long, Great Lakes
Historical Society, Vermillion, Ohio 10/9/1991
Phone conversation with John Polliseck, GLMI
10/9/1991

TOWARD THE SOUNDS OF DISASTER
REF; Bay City Tribune 7/13/1909
Bay City Times 7/13/1909
"Namesakes 1900-1909"," 1910-1919," Greenwood
"Great Lakes Ships We Remember II," Van der Linden
"The Discovery Of The John McGean," Trotter; The
Telescope Jan.-Feb. 1989

LOST 'N FOUND, 'N LOST
REF; Bay City Tribune 5/7/1901, 11/12,13,15/1901
    Bay City Times-Press 11/ 13,14,15,16,18/1901
        "Munising Shipwrecks," Stonehouse
        "Namesakes, 1900-1909,1910-1919,1920-1929."
    Greenwood
        "A Pictorial History of the Great Lakes," Hatcher &
Walter
        "Shipwrecks Of The Lakes," Bowen
        "Shipwrecks Of Lake Huron," Parker
        Beeson's Marine Directory 1902
        "River District Bicentennial Photo Collection,"
The Marine City Rotary Club, 1976

A NEW WARDROBE FOR MRS. RUSSELL
REF;   Bay City Tribune 8/8,9/1912
        "Namesakes II," Greenwood
        "Namesakes 1910-1919," Greenwood
        Beeson's Marine Directory 1913
        "The Life and Times of The Bessemer Fleet," G. P.
Bugbee; Telescope, March-April 1978
        "The Smallest 500-footers" G. Dewar; Telescope,
July-August 1990
        "Lake Huron, The American Lakes Series," Landon
        "Lake Superior, The American Lakes Series," Nute

MATE LEBOEUF'S PERSONAL DISASTER
REF; Beeson's Marine Directory 1913
        "Namesakes II," Greenwood
        "Namesakes 1910-1919," Greenwood
        "A Pictorial History of the Great Lakes," Hatcher &
Walter

GUNDERSEN'S ISLAND
REF; Saginaw Evening News 10/23/1905
    "Namesakes 1910-1919," Greenwood
    "The Great Lakes Car Ferries," Walker
    "Ghost Ships Of The Great Lakes," Boyer
    Photos of the John V. Jones; The Great Lakes
Marine Collection, Milwaukee Public Library

CHIEF GIBSON'S POST
REF; Bay City Times 5/25,26/1910
    Sault Saint Marie Evening News 5/24,25/1910
    "Namesakes 1910-1919," Greenwood
    "Namesakes II," Greenwood
    "Shipwrecks Of Lake Huron," Parker
    Letter from Vi Bassett, 10/19/1990

HOODOOS, MISTAKEN IDENTITIES AND A CAPTAIN'S TALE
REF; Bay City Tribune 5/7/1901, 11/15,16/1904
    Sault Saint Marie Evening News 11/11/1904
    Bay City Times 8/8/1924
    "Namesakes 1900-1909,1910-1919,1920-1929"
Greenwood
    "Namesakes II," Greenwood
    "Shipwrecks Of Lake Huron," Parker
    "Lake Erie, The American Lakes Series," Hatcher
    "Freshwater Whales," Wright
    "Great Lakes Ships We Remember,I,II" Van der Linden
    Beeson's Marine Directory, 1905
    "Locks and ships," Soo Locks Boat Tours
    "Stormy Seas," Wes Oleszewski
    Phone conversation with David Trotter, 7/25/1991
    Phone conversation with David Barilovich 9/12/1991

A DEAL'S A DEAL
Ref; Bay City Tribune, 11/22/1907
      "Namesakes 1910-1919," Greenwood
      "Great Lakes Ships We Remember II," Van der Linden
      Beeson's Marine Directory, 1902
      "Lake Erie, The American Lakes Series," Hatcher
THE KETCHAM BLOCKADE
REF; Bay City Tribune 5/24/1910, 6/4,9,12/1910
      Sault Saint Marie Evening News 5/21,23,24,27/1910
      "Namesakes 1900-1909,1910-1919,1920-1929"
Greenwood
      "Namesakes II," Greenwood
      "Great Lakes Ships We Remember,I,II" Van der
Linden
      "Locks and Ships," Soo Locks Boat Tours
      "The `Yellow' Kid And Her Kid Sisters, Part II"
Dewar, Telescope; March-April 1987
      "Lake Erie, The American Lakes Series," Hatcher
      "Lake Superior, The American Lakes Series," Nute
      "True Tales Of The Great Lakes," Boyer
      "Shipwrecks Of The Great Lakes," Bowen
      Phone conversation with David Barilovich 9/12/1991
      Tape recording of vessel traffic 9/18/1988, myself

TAWAS POINT AND VESSELS GONE BY
REF; Bay City Tribune 7/2/1890
    Bay City Tribune, 11/20,22,23,24/1907
    Bay City Times, 6/14/ 1931
      Green's Marine Directory, 1919
      Beeson's Marine Directory, 1908
      "Great Lakes Ships We Remember, I, II" Van der
Linden
      "Namesakes 1900-1909," Greenwood
      "Shipwrecks of Lake Huron," Parker

Acknowledgements

Without the help of many people this text would have been less than full, so the following is the least that I can do in expressing my appreciation.

First of all, gratitude must go to shipwreck author and historian Frederick Stonehouse. With the aid of his insight and straightforward evaluation of my first book, I was able to more carefully shape this text. There is nothing that a person in my profession appreciates more than an honest critique, with no axe to grind.

I wish to thank my fellow boat-nut D. J. Story, who took the time to dig into a century of newspapers to find the obscure information that saved two chapters in this book. Of course, D. J.'s wife Penny had to step in at one point to rescue us both.

Thanks must go out to Great Lakes Historians and Researchers Martha Long of the Great Lakes Historical Society, John Polliseck of the Great Lakes Maritime Institute, Sandy Broder of the Milwaukee Public Library, Ruthann Beck of Thunder Bay Divers and, most prominently, famed research diver David Trotter. Thank yous to some who found me in their way but were helpful none the less, and thanks to Mac Eagle who gave up the only printing micro-film machine at the Bayliss Library so that I could burn off two chapters' worth of copies. Vi Bassette sent a helpful letter that solved my dilemma involving her family tree and I thank her. Gratitude to Hydraulic Engineer Dave Barilovich of the Army Corps of Engineers for insight into the construction of the Rock Cut, Gordon Crago for high-tech computer scanning and donations, my sister-in-law Karen for typing in my absence and to the countless others whom I have met and received encouragement from.

Thanks to Maryjean McKelvy for her invaluable aid in editing the final draft.

Acknowledgements

Warmest thanks to my family—my wife Teresa for her endless patience and support, and my parents, sister, brother and in-laws who are my best marketers.

Finally I would like to break again with "proper" literary style, to thank Anita and the gang at Avery Color Studios for taking a chance on a complete unknown, with a text that became "Stormy Seas". With their support, I will continue to tell the true-to-life tales of the Great Lakes oreboats.

About the Author

W. Wes Oleszewski was born in Saginaw, Michigan in 1957 and grew up in the Tri-Cities area. His interest in the Great Lakes and the oreboats that sail upon them grew up with him, as he watched them pass along the Saginaw River. When he started into the aviation career field in 1977, he took up Great Lakes maritime history as a hobby. This led to the development of a personal research library, and a fleet of some 40 miniature radio controlled oreboats. In 1982, he joined the Great Lakes Maritime Institute, and the Saginaw River Marine Historical Society in 1988.

While going through the book section of a Saginaw maritime gift store in 1986, he found that there were some relatively new books out on Great Lakes vessels, but for the most part they were just gatherings of data. Either that, or the texts concerned involved the facts about the same two dozen or so shipwrecks. It seemed no one was telling the tales anymore, so Wes took it upon himself to tell the stories of the forgotten boats. In 1987 he finished his first book, and in 1990 it was published as "Stormy Seas, Triumphs and Tragedies of Great Lakes Ships". Before the first book hit the presses he had already started work on this text and as of this writing work is underway on his third book.

A graduate of the Embry Riddle Aeronautical University, Wes earned a Bachelor of Science Degree in Aeronautical Science. He holds a multi-engine instrument commercial pilot's certificate and flight instructor certificates, and he is currently engaged in a career as a professional pilot.

Index of Vessels

We at Avery Color Studios thank you for purchasing this book. We hope it has provided many hours of enjoyable reading.

Learn more about Michigan and the Great Lakes area through a broad range of titles that cover mining and logging days, early Indians and their legends, Great Lakes shipwrecks, Cully Gage's Northwoods Readers (full of laughter and occasional sadness), and full-color pictorials of days gone by and the natural beauty of this land. Beautiful note stationery is also available.

For a free catalog, please call 800-722-9925 in Michigan or 906/226-3338, or tear out this page and mail it to us. Please tape or staple the card and put a stamp on it.

PLEASE RETURN TO:

COLOR STUDIOS

P.O. Box 308
Marquette MI 49855

CALL TOLL FREE
1-800-722-9925

Your complete shipping address:

_____

_____

_____

_____

Fold, Staple, Affix Stamp and Mail

_____

_____

_____

_____

COLOR STUDIOS

P.O. Box 308
Marquette MI 49855